THE

Bride

RENEWING OUR PASSION
FOR THE CHURCH

FORMERLY TITLED *RISE & SHINE*

CHARLES R. SWINDOLL

ZondervanPublishingHouse

Grand Rapids, Michigan

A Division of HarperCollinsPublishers

The Bride
Copyright © 1994 by Charles R. Swindoll

Requests for information should be addressed to:
Zondervan Publishing House
Grand Rapids, Michigan 49530

Library of Congress Cataloging-in-Publication Data

Swindoll, Charles R. The bride: renewing our passion for the church / Charles R.
Swindoll. p. cm. Originally published: *Rise & Shine*. Portland, Or.: Multnomah c1989.
Includes bibliographical references and index.

ISBN 0-310-42070-9
1. Mission of the church.   2. Christian life — 1960- .   I. Title.
[BV601.8.S87   1994]   253 – dc20
                                                             94-536
                                                             CIP

Unless otherwise indicated, all Scripture references are from the New American Standard
Bible, © The Lockman Foundation 1960, 1962, 1963, 1968, 1971, 1972, 1973, 1975, 1977.
Used by permission.

Scripture references marked TLB are from The Living Bible, copyright 1971 by Tyndale
House Publishers, Wheaton, Ill. Used by permission.

Scripture references marked Phillips are from J. B. Phillips: The New Testament in Modern
English, revised edition. © J. B. Phillips 1958, 1960, 1972. Used by permission of Macmillan
Publishing Co., Inc.

Scripture references marked Moffat are from The Bible: A New Translation, copyright
1922, 1924, 1925, 1926, 1936 by Harper & Row, Publishers, Inc.; copyright 1950, 1952,
1953, 1954 by James A. R. Moffatt.

Cover design by Multnomah Graphics

Printed in the United States of America

94 95 96 97 98 99 00 / ❖ DH / 10 9 8 7 6 5 4 3 2 1

This edition is printed on acit-free paper and meets the American National Standards
Institute Z39.48 standard.

This book is dedicated to

KENNETH P. MEBERG, PH.D.

whose close friendship, wise counsel, and insightful ideas,
many years ago as I was getting under way at the First
Evangelical Free Church of Fullerton, proved invaluable
when we grew and multiplied. As that congregation reaps
the dividends of his investment of time and energy,
I thank God upon every remembrance of my friend.

I am the first to see her when she appears at the back of the church. But she snaps heads sidewards with every row she passes.

That's the way it is with the bride. She remains hidden from friends and relatives inside the church until the playing of the four-measure fanfare of Wagner's *Wedding March*. Then the notes of the fanfare sound. She steps out in view of all of us who face the congregation. Row by row, people turn to face the center aisle. They gasp, they cry, they laugh, they beam, they rejoice.

The bride stands us on our heads. She is the center of the wedding and radiates every hope and dream on that day.

Maybe that's why God chose the symbol of the Bride to represent the church. Christ meant for His church to turn heads, to turn the world upside down, and to draw attention to itself as the location of hope and belief in a world shot through with cynicism.

Jesus was forever talking about weddings (Matthew 22:1–14; Matthew 25:1–13; Luke 12:35–36; Luke 14:7–11; John 2:1–11). The fact is God referred to the people of Israel as His Bride in the Old Testament (Hosea 2:19–20). Later Jesus told many stories about wedding feasts, fathers of bridegrooms, seating arrangements, miraculous caterings, and so projected on the biblical screen the pictures of a wedding and Himself as the Bridegroom. Then New Testament writers named the church as the Bride. And in the last few pages of the Bible, the final and biggest wedding of all time takes place, with all assembled and all rejoicing. Jesus Christ, the Lamb of God, and His Bride, the church, will close out recorded time with a wedding celebration that will make New Year's Eve in Times Square look like a wienie roast in Alpena, Michigan. (My apologies to Alpena.)

After spending more than thirty years in the pastorate, I've come to a startling conclusion. We the church have almost forgotten who we are—the Bride of Christ. That means we've almost forgotten what powerful things we can do as we stand beside our omnipotent Partner. In the pages that follow I want to call us back to our role. We've drifted as the church because of feelings of weakness, aimlessness, and a lack of destiny. It's time we remember again.

We who comprise the century-twenty body of Christ are living in some of the most (if not *the* most) significant years in the history of Christendom. Opportunities in the international scene are expanding and exciting. The privilege of evangelizing the lost and spreading the message of hope and encouragement to the saved has greater potential than ever. None can deny that our Lord's return is closer than it has ever been before. In many places around the world Christianity is on the rise.

Yet, strangely, many in His church seem to have lost perspective. Longtime values are eroding. Small-time skirmishes and petty infighting within our own ranks are draining too much of our energy. Instead of fulfilling our clearly defined God-given mandate, a large number of Christians have set their sights on myopic and selfish involvements. Instant gratification is fast replacing eternal goals. God's stated action plan for the church is being eclipsed by a man-made assortment of activities that ranges from the spurious to the scandalous.

If the apostles, who drew the first maps to guide us on our way across the uncertain seas of the centuries, and if the Reformers, who built many of the vessels in which we were to travel, were to return as Rip van Winkle of old and see the plight in which we find ourselves, I believe their mouths would drop open and they would stare in disbelief. Some would surely wonder if we had misplaced the map—or lost sight of the destination and chosen to dive in and swim in different directions.

This book, though brief and perhaps oversimplified, is a sincere attempt on my part to give us a good look at the Bride and help us understand what the church should be. In doing so, I am deliberately not dealing with some of the current social and religious con-

cerns that grab the attention of the public and often wind up in the headlines or courts of our land. Neither do I address various styles of church government, which have been sufficiently written about for the past decade. The issues I address are far more basic and clearly defined. Best of all, my suggestions are attainable. Having been in the pastorate for almost three decades, I have had ample opportunities to put them to the test. They work.

This book is not a series of impractical and idealistic theories but of biblical and realistic essentials. But don't be deceived into thinking they are easily achieved. Each will require an enormous amount of discernment and discipline, neither of which is popular in a generation that has preferred quick imitations instead of the real thing. Perhaps I should repeat that every answer I present, every suggestion I offer, is sourced in Scripture, the only inerrant source document God has endorsed.

So, if you are tired of theories that sound pious but lack relevance, if you are ready to think through key issues and the scriptural principles that bear upon them, if you have had your fill of passive dreams and foggy goals, if you're ready to get involved in God's action plan . . . this is your kind of book. Understand, it won't accomplish the objectives for you, but it will alert you to what needs to be done. It's a shrill sound in the night, not a soft tap on the shoulder. It may not spell out all the details, but at least it's sufficient to get you out of a slumber mode and into action.

I've never been interested in simply giving folks "something to think about." Seems to me we've gathered enough dust sitting around merely discussing our plight. What turns my crank is motivating people with the truth of Scripture, then seeing them get in gear. The recent three-word advertisement for Nike athletic shoes says it best: JUST DO IT.

My heartfelt thanks go to my family members and to the staff and congregation of the First Evangelical Free Church of Fullerton. These two sides of my life have held me accountable and helped me remain in touch. It has been in the day-to-day laboratory of both these worlds that I have been able to turn theory into reality.

There's an urgency about the church's understanding its role as Christ's Bride. Without her, the Bridegroom will not be seen—until He comes again. But I think God has a better plan. And it will turn some heads around.

Chuck Swindoll
Fullerton, California

"Let us rejoice and be glad and give the glory to Him,
for the marriage of the Lamb has come
and His bride has made herself ready."
(Revelation 19:7)

And He [God] put all things in subjection under His [Christ's] feet,
and gave Him as head over all things to the church,
which is His body, the fulness of Him who fills all in all.
(Ephesians 1:22–23)

This mystery is great;
but I am speaking with reference
to Christ and the church.
(Ephesians 5:32)

CHAPTER ONE

OUR PURPOSE

I am told that Socrates was considered wise, not because he knew all the right answers but because he knew how to ask the right questions.

Questions—the right questions—can be penetrating, leading to revealing answers. They can expose hidden motives as well as enable us to face truth we had not admitted even to ourselves.

The Book of Questions, by Dr. Gregory Stock, is one of those volumes I find difficult to put aside. It includes almost 275 thought-provoking questions that pull us out of our shell. You find yourself unable to hide or dodge the uncomfortable. Want some examples?

- If you were to die this evening with no opportunity to communicate with anyone, what would you most regret not having told someone? Why haven't you told them yet?

- You discover your wonderful one-year-old child is, because of a mix-up at the hospital, not yours. Would you want to exchange the child to try to correct the mistake?

- If you could use a voodoo doll to hurt anyone you chose, would you?

- Your house, containing everything you own, catches fire. After saving your loved ones and pets, you have time to safely make a final dash and save any one item. What would it be?

- While parking late at night, you slightly scrape the side of a Porsche. You are certain no one else is aware of what happened. The damage is minor and would be covered by insurance. Would you leave a note? [1]

Not long ago I read about a fellow who really did that—except people *were* watching. As they looked on, he took out a piece of paper and wrote the following message:

A number of people around me think I'm leaving you a note that includes my name and address, but I am not.

He carefully folded the paper, stuck it under the car's windshield wiper, smiled at those watching, then quickly drove away. Dirty dog! Here are a couple more:

- If you found that a good friend had AIDS, would you avoid him? What if your brother or sister had it?

- If you were at a friend's house for Thanksgiving dinner and you found a dead cockroach in the salad, what would you do? [2]

Funny thing about questions, they force us to come to terms with the issue. I found it interesting that the least-asked questions in Stock's book were the "Why" questions. Yet those are the most critical. They don't mess around; they go right to the heart of an issue.

The other day I pulled from my shelf one of the largest reference books in my study. It's a foot tall, about two inches thick, and very heavy. It is my exhaustive biblical concordance—an alphabetical listing of every word in the Bible. Out of curiosity I turned to the

"W" section and checked the term *"Why."* To my surprise I found almost five tiny-print columns of my concordance dedicated just to the *"Why"* questions found in the Bible.

Here is a random sampling of several of them.

God asked Cain, *"Why* are you angry?"

The angels asked Abram, *"Why* did Sarah laugh?"

Moses asked himself, *"Why* is the bush not burned up?"

Nathan, when confronting David, asked, *"Why* have you despised the word of the Lord?"

Job asked God, *"Why* did I not die at birth?"

The *"Why"* question seemed to be Jesus' favorite. He was the One who asked:

"Why do you worry?"

"Why do you look at the speck in your brother's eye and not at the log in your own eye?"

"Why do you call Me 'Lord, Lord' and don't do what I say?"

"Why do you not believe Me?"

One of His last statements on the cross was a *"Why"* question, *"Why* have You forsaken Me?"

The angels met those coming to the empty tomb with the question, *"Why* do you seek the living among the dead?"

THE PRIMARY PURPOSE

To arrive at the foundational reason the church exists, you have to ask *"Why?"*

Why, indeed, has the church been called into existence? **Why** does a church building occupy a piece of property on the corner? **Why** have we erected walls and a roof over the buildings in which we meet? **Why** do we engage in a ministry of music? **Why** are sermons preached? **Why** do we support the work of the church with our funds? **Why** do we send missionaries around the world?

If you or I were to ask those questions next Sunday, we would hear a lot of answers—many of them good—but I doubt they would represent the primary purpose.

Here are some of the answers we would be given:

- To present the gospel to the lost.

- To have an opportunity for regular worship and instruction.

- To bring hope to the hurting.

- To be a lighthouse in the community.

- To equip saints for the work of ministry.

- To declare and support wholesome values (home, moral and ethical purity, the dignity of individuals, godly living, healthy marriages, integrity, etc.).

- To send the gospel around the world through missionary efforts.

- To reach today's youth and challenge them to make Christ the center of their lives, their choice of a career, their plans for the future.

- To pray.

- To build up the saints.

- To comfort the grieving; encourage the lonely; feed the hungry; minister to the handicapped; and help the aged, the abused, and the confused.

- To stimulate action and involvement in critical social issues.

- To model a standard of authentic righteousness.

- To teach the Scriptures with a view to holy living.

Each of these reasons is valid, wholesome, and worthwhile. The church must certainly be engaged in those activities. But not one is absolutely primary. Nothing in that list states the foundational purpose for the church's existence. Amazing, isn't it? All these years we have been involved in the work of the church, yet very few know why . . . I mean the taproot reason why.

What then is that primary purpose? We find the answer clearly stated in the New Testament letter of First Corinthians. For many of us, seeing this truth in its simplicity and boldness will be as refreshing and startling as the first sight of the bride on wedding day. Yet the better we understand it, the more we will realize our purpose personally as Christians and corporately as a church. The Holy Spirit led the great apostle Paul to write,

> *Whether, then, you eat or drink or whatever you do, do all to the* **glory of God** (1 Corinthians 10:31).

In the simplest of terms, there's our answer to why we exist. The church's primary purpose is to glorify the Lord our God. May we never again forget it, though we often have in the past.

Look at how broadly Paul puts it, "WHETHER. . . ." Whether we are eating or drinking, hurting or helping, serving or struggling. The activities are limitless, but the purpose remains the same.

Look further: "WHATEVER. . . ." Again, it is as broad as we wish to make it. Whatever you are personally—male or female; adult or youth or child; in whatever country you find yourself; in whatever circumstance—the goal is God's greater glory. Let's wake up to our purpose! In another brilliant flash of scriptural wisdom, the apostle Paul ends a prayer of thanks to God saying, "To Him be the glory in the church and in Christ Jesus to all generations forever and ever. Amen" (Ephesians 3:21). The word "glory" continues to get maximum visibility in these pages I'm writing. For good reason. It is our ultimate purpose. Paul is saying that glory goes to God by way of the church and Christ. And this is the Bride and Bridegroom combination I have been talking about from the beginning of the book.

A few chapters earlier in the same first-century letter to the Corinthians we find this probing question:

> *Or do you not know that your body is a temple of the Holy Spirit who is in you, whom you have from God, and that you are not your own?* (6:19).

Did you realize that? His reason for asking such a question is set forth in the next statement:

For you have been bought with a price: therefore glorify God in your body (6:20).

There it is again. God is concerned that we glorify Him even in our body. The way we treat it. What we put into it. What we allow it to say. Where we go with it. How much rest we provide it. How well we keep it fit. Whatever you do with your body, make sure that your physical existence brings glory to God.

The fifteenth chapter of the previous letter, Romans, includes a couple of verses that sound a lot like what we've been reading.

Now may the God who gives perseverance and encouragement grant you to be of the same mind with one another according to Christ Jesus; that with one accord you may with one voice glorify the God and Father of our Lord Jesus Christ (vv. 5–6).

The Bible is *full* of statements like this. Our sole purpose, our basic reason for existence, is to bring maximum glory to our God. Scripture virtually pulsates with the mandate, "Glorify God!"

Somehow we have slept through the repeated reminders. In our day of fragile egos and Madison Avenue-style religion, it is easy to lose our way and to imagine the church's primary goal is to get bigger, to build massive edifices, to double our attendance every three years or so. A growing church has become the envy of those that aren't.

Another popular purpose is to make an impression, to look good . . . or to have great sermons, provide good music, and on and on and on. Understand that there is nothing wrong with any of those things as long as they are done with the right motive and kept in perspective. But my point is this: *They are not primary.*

To make all this extremely practical, the question needs to be asked on a regular basis: Why am I doing this? Why did I say yes? Why did I agree to that? Why am I teaching? Why do I sing in the choir? Why am I so involved in this adult fellowship? Why do I plan in my budget to give this amount of money? Why? Why? WHY? When those questions are asked, there must be one and only one answer: *To glorify God.*

While on this subject, let's consider another Scripture, 2 Thessalonians 1:11–12:

To this end also we pray for you always that our God may count you worthy of your calling, and fulfill every desire for goodness and the work of faith with power; in order that the name of our Lord Jesus may be glorified in you, and you in Him, according to the grace of our God and the Lord Jesus Christ.

Interesting response, isn't it? As you glorify the Lord God, you'll be glorified in Him. You will find that it is catching. When you glorify God, it has a healthy impact on others. They will see your model and want to glorify Him as well. Our Lord Jesus taught:

Let your light shine before men in such a way that they may see your good works, and glorify your Father who is in heaven (Matthew 5:16).

If your life is an example of glorifying God, others won't see your good works and glorify *you*, because they'll know what you are doing is for God's glory. I'm not able to explain how they can tell. I just know they can. It's remarkable how pride can ooze out of the flesh and display itself, prompting others to glorify the person. But when there is glory given to God and the action is done solely for His glory, somehow people can tell—and they direct their gratitude and praise back to God. It's a chain reaction that leads to a beautiful expression of spontaneous worship.

All this may seem so surprising you are inclined to think it is a new concept. Yet it is as ancient as Scripture.

Well, then, is it new in church history? No, it is as old as the *Westminster Shorter Catechism*, devised in 1647. Remember the first question the Scottish Presbyterians were to ask young students learning theology at the feet of their teachers?

Question: What is the chief end of man?

Answer: Man's chief end is to glorify God and to enjoy Him forever.[3]

AN ANALYSIS OF THE ANSWER

Let's analyze that statement. I can write about glory for several pages, but because the term seems abstract, a little oblique, we may not understand what it means. We know *generally* what it means, but we need to be very specific if we hope to model it.

When I study the Scriptures, I find that glory is used in three major ways. First of all, glory refers to light, the light of God's presence, a bright and shining light from heaven. This expression of the glory of God appears in Exodus 40:34, where we read: ". . . the glory of the LORD filled the tabernacle."

I cannot fully imagine what it looked like, but it must have been a blinding light. Because of its presence, the Hebrews knew God was present. He also appeared before them in their wilderness journey in the form of a cloud by day and a massive pillar of fire by night. But when the tabernacle's construction was finished and God's presence rested in the holiest of all, it came in the form of a brilliant, searing light called the "shekinah" of God. So awesome was the light that to step into it inappropriately meant sudden death.

Continuing our search through Scripture, we find a second and equally significant use of glory. In 1 Corinthians chapter 15, we find there is a glory that refers to a unique representation or distinctive appearance, used of the celestial bodies.

> *All flesh is not the same flesh, but there is one flesh of men, and another flesh of beasts, and another flesh of birds, and another of fish. There are also heavenly bodies and earthly bodies, but the glory of the heavenly is one, and the glory of the earthly is another. There is one glory of the sun, and another glory of the moon, and another glory of the stars; for star differs from star in glory* (15:39–41).

How intriguing! There's something about the stellar spaces that represents a particular kind of glory. Those stars and suns and planets bear an appearance that reveals a distinctive and awesome glory. But when it comes to the goals of our lives or the purpose of the church, we're not talking about either a brilliant light or the distinct representation of glory in earthly or heavenly bodies.

When referring to the church's bottom-line purpose, *that* glory means to magnify, to elevate, to shed radiance or splendor on Another.

So what does it mean for the church or for each individual Christian to glorify God? It means to magnify, exalt, and elevate the Lord our God as we humble ourselves and defer to His wisdom, His authority.

It was beautifully illustrated in John the Baptizer, who once said, "He must increase, but I must decrease" (John 3:30). What a wonderful model John was! John was only the voice, but he exalted Jesus as the Word. John called himself a lamp; but to him, Jesus was the Light. John was only a man, Jesus was the Messiah. John willingly lost his congregation to the Lord. They all followed Jesus . . . and John *wanted* it that way. In fact, when asked his identity by the priests and Levites, the dialogue that followed was revealing:

> *John replied . . . "I am A VOICE OF ONE CRYING IN THE WILDERNESS, 'MAKE STRAIGHT THE WAY OF THE LORD,' as Isaiah the prophet said." Now they had been sent from the Pharisees. And they asked him, and said to him, "Why then are you baptizing, if you are not the Christ, nor Elijah, nor the Prophet?" John answered them saying, "I baptize in water, but among you stands One whom you do not know. It is He who comes after me, the thong of whose sandal I am not worthy to untie"* (John 1:23–27).

Not once did the Baptizer seek the glory that belonged only to the Messiah. In his own words, he considered himself unworthy even to loosen the leather thong on Messiah's sandal. All this leads me to believe something I have never heard anyone develop, even though it is woven through the whole of Scripture: *I cannot at the same time accept the glory and give God the glory.* I cannot at the same time expect and enjoy the glory if I determine at the same moment to give Him the glory. Glorifying God means being occupied with and committed to His ways rather than preoccupied with and determined to go my own way. It is being so thrilled with Him, so devoted to Him, so committed to Him that we cannot get enough of Him!

Isaiah 55 is a wonderful chapter of Scripture. It is not addressed to people who are satisfied with a little sip of God, a tiny taste. It is an invitation to those who are thirsty for Him . . . who are ready to gulp down all that God has. That is why the prophet begins, "Ho!" (Listen up, everybody! Pay close attention!)

> *HO! Every one who thirsts, come to the waters; And you who have no money come, buy and eat* (v. 1).

Understand that this is not literal water. Nor is it literal money. This is beautiful Hebrew poetry, so don't make it walk literally on all fours. Read it with the heart of a poet.

> *Come, buy wine and milk*
> *Without money and without cost.*
> *Why do you spend money for what is not bread,*
> *And your wages for what does not satisfy?*

(There's a another "why?" question worth pursuing.)

> *Listen carefully to Me, and eat what is good,*
> *And delight yourself in abundance.*

Now, read carefully the next four verses:

> *Seek the LORD while He may be found;*
> *Call upon Him while He is near.*
> *Let the wicked forsake his way,*
> *And the unrighteous man his thoughts;*
> *And let him return to the LORD,*
> *And He will have compassion on him;*
> *And to our God,*
> *For He will abundantly pardon.*
> *For My thoughts are not your thoughts . . .* (vv. 6–9).

Is it possible to run a "church operation" that will have public appeal and gather a crowd and keep people coming? I hope to shout! We can do all the slick things that work in the world system and get the same results—it will bring folks out from under the rocks! If you don't believe that, you haven't watched some of the religious television programs that follow that style—most of them with a huge viewing audience. The next time you watch, deliberately ask yourself, "Who's getting the glory in this ministry?" You see, if we do ministry *our* way, it won't be for His glory, because (as we just read) our ways are not His ways. His ways are so much higher and purer and strangely invisible that when we finally decide to conduct a church His way, the world will literally sit up and take notice. The sudden contrast, the uniqueness will astound them. The awesome glory of God will be all the appeal that will be needed to create an interest in spiritual things.

David, in Psalm 145, wrote of this in a little different manner. Try to imagine a congregation committed to this kind of worship—where exalting the living Lord is literally their greatest delight.

> I will extol Thee, my God, O King;
> And I will bless Thy name forever and ever.
> Every day I will bless Thee,
> And I will praise Thy name forever and ever.
> Great is the LORD, and highly to be praised;
> And His greatness is unsearchable.
> One generation shall praise Thy works to another,
> And shall declare Thy mighty acts.
> On the glorious splendor of Thy majesty,
> And on Thy wonderful works, I will meditate.
> And men shall speak of the power of Thine awesome acts;
> And I will tell of Thy greatness.
> They shall eagerly utter the memory of Thine abundant goodness,
> And shall shout joyfully of Thy righteousness (vv. 1–7).

These are the words of a man who truly understood what it meant to give God the glory. Would that all God's ministers were cut from the same piece of cloth!

Things were not as good for David in Psalm 86. The bottom seems to have dropped out of his life. In this psalm, he is on the bottom looking up. He is the same man addressing the same God, but affliction and trouble have come aboard. Yet this ancient song is written in the same spirit of praise. Circumstances did not change his style.

Incline Thine ear, O LORD, and answer me;
For I am afflicted and needy.
Do preserve my soul, for I am a godly man;
O Thou my God, save Thy servant who trusts in Thee.
Be gracious to me, O Lord,
For to Thee I cry all day long.
Make glad the soul of Thy servant,
For to Thee, O Lord, I lift up my soul.
For Thou, Lord, art good, and ready to forgive,
And abundant in lovingkindness
to all who call upon Thee.
Give ear, O LORD, to my prayer;
And give heed to the voice of my supplications!
In the day of my trouble I shall call upon Thee,
For Thou wilt answer me.
There is no one like Thee among the gods, O Lord;
Nor are there any works like Thine.
All nations whom Thou hast made shall come and worship
*   before Thee, O Lord;*
And they shall glorify Thy name.
For Thou art great and doest wondrous deeds;
Thou alone art God (Psalm 86:1–10).

I love the man's consistency. Whether in days of delight (Psalm 145) or days of distress (Psalm 86), the glory went to the Lord, his God. Don't you appreciate those final words: "Thou alone art God"?

How Does All This Apply?

Allow me to spend the balance of this first chapter analyzing the importance of glorifying God on a *personal* basis. All of this could apply to the church in general, but it will help us grasp the concept better if we study its importance in our individual Christian lives. When we finally see and embrace our purpose for existence, we come to the realization that glorifying God applies to every detail of living. Let's start with the "whens" in life.

When I am unsure, I glorify Him by seeking His will and then waiting for His guidance. When I need to make a decision, I lean on His Word for direction and His Spirit for strength. Some examples? You name it: selecting a job, finding a place to live, determining which car to drive, focusing on a goal to accomplish. I decide on each one of those things only for His glory. How about this one? When affliction and suffering assault me. Or, when pursuing an education—all for His glory, not mine. The same applies to the school I attend, the courses I take, the degree I pursue, the career I ultimately embrace. When any subject surfaces that calls for my response, His glory is to be in my attitude and woven through my answer. When I am thinking and planning. When I win or lose. When I must relinquish a dream or realize it is best to walk away without fighting for my rights, I willingly surrender.

Why? Again, the same answer—*for His glory.*

Next, let's apply this to the "ins" in life. In my public life or private affairs, I seek His glory. In relationships that please me or challenge me, they are all for His glory. In my home, in my work, in my school, in traveling as well as in being alone as I occupy a small, monotonous, and inconspicuous place. In my research, my studies, my academic assignments, my preparation for exams, my taking of exams, my receiving a grade, and my practicing a profession—all for His glory. In fame and fortune, public applause and appreciation, as well as in those days when all that fades, it is all, I repeat, *for His glory.*

Let's take this one step further to include all the "ifs" in life. If a person I love stays or leaves, God gets the glory. If a cause I support captures the hearts of others or goes down in flames, God gets the glory. If the plans I arrange succeed or fail or must be altered, I focus on His being glorified, regardless. If the church I am involved in grows or stops growing, God gets the glory. If, as a pastor, it means my leaving to make room for the right person, God gets the glory. If it means my staying in spite of the odds, God gets the glory.

My permanent theme in life? "To God be the glory for the things He has done."[4]

How Does It Occur?

You knew we would finally arrive at this question, didn't you? How do we make all this happen?

Obviously, you can't accomplish your purpose simply by reading this chapter over and over again. That won't help you, not in the long run. If I'm reading your mind correctly, your interest is in personalizing this truth so effectively that you end your life like Jesus, who said at the end of His, "I glorified Thee on the earth" (John 17:4a). He summed up His whole life in those six wonderful words. The question is, how can we do the same?

At the risk of oversimplification, I want to make three suggestions to help make that happen. Trust me, they are both realistic and attainable. How does glorifying God occur?

First: *By cultivating the habit of including the Lord God in every segment of your life.*

This is to be a conscious and constant thought. Habits are formed that way. It may help to write this probing question on several three-by-five cards: IS GOD GETTING THE GLORY? Put a card on the visor of your car, another under the glass at your desk, a third one on the mirror in your bathroom, and another in front of the sink where the dishes are done or at the stove where meals are cooked. *Is God getting the glory?* Am I giving God glory for this moment?

I appreciate Richard Bube's words:

> Man cannot serve both self and God. The corruption of human nature produces a self-will which turns man against God and glorifies human ability rather than God's grace. Pride and selfishness are the characteristics of human nature which demands its own way in all things. The first step toward serving God as He would have us serve Him, therefore, requires that we constantly and consciously put down the demands of self and surrender our desires to the Lord.[5]

I remember almost as if it were last week the day it dawned on me that my Christianity was not limited to Sundays. It was a wrap-around lifestyle. Sunday just happened to be one of the seven days each week it impacted me. It is possible that you have yet to make a definite step toward glorifying God in your work or in your relationship with your roommate at school or your mate at home. I urge you to open every closet, every room in your life, and allow God's glory in. How does it occur?

Second: *By refusing to expect or accept any of the glory that belongs to God.*

Read that again . . . this time more slowly, more thoughtfully. It is helpful to remember that the flesh (your carnal nature) is very creative and selfish. Think of it as a huge sponge, ready and willing to soak up all the glory. It is a great pretender, acting like it is humble, yet all the while loving the strokes. It anticipates them. It is ambitious. It is energetic. It looks for opportunities to grab the glory that belongs to God alone. The flesh is not choosy. It doesn't mind getting the glory for spiritual-sounding things or religious acts. Who knows how many sermons have been preached in the flesh? I've certainly done a few, I must confess. Furthermore, by hiding my motives, I can, with public skill, manipulate a congregation to do a number of things I want done. And I can gloss it over so effectively they will think they are doing it God's way, for God's purpose, when in actuality they are doing *my* will, and *I* get the glory. I can actually take the glory God alone deserves.

I'm suggesting a better way—that we no longer expect or accept any of the glory that belongs to God. His glory is His alone, so let's be sure He gets it all from now on! Again, how does it occur?

Third: *By maintaining a priority relationship with Him that is more important than any other on earth.*

You may be closer to your child than you are to God. You may spend more time with your wife or husband than you ever have with God. You could be more concerned about your family's safety and future happiness and ultimate welfare than you are about the will of God in your own personal life. Nothing wrong with loving your family or planning for their future, but if it is your sincere desire to glorify God, then I need to remind you that He expects to have a priority relationship. The same could be said of any other earthly relationship that has become so strong it competes with your relationship with Him. If I correctly understand the teachings of Jesus regarding a relationship with Him, He's saying the relationship with the living God is so important nothing can come between it or ahead of it. Nothing.

The denial of self is a difficult assignment. Ideally, we learn it at home. Some time ago I finished Douglas Southall Freeman's classic biography of the famous confederate general, Robert E. Lee. The book is titled simply *Lee*. Toward the end of the book, this eloquent paragraph appears:

> Of humility and submission was born a spirit of self-denial that prepared him for the hardships of the war and, still more, for the dark destitution, the spiritual counterpart of the social self-control his mother had inculcated in his boyhood days, and it grew in power throughout his life. . . . A young mother brought her baby to him to be blessed. He took the infant in his arms and looked at it and then at her and slowly said, "Teach him he must deny himself."[6]

We're back to the Baptizer's credo: "He must increase, but I must decrease." It must be for His glory, not mine. Rather than running ahead to get my own way, He must be first. I must be diminished, He must be lifted up. For His glory, I must take whatever position He appoints for me. I'm the servant, He is Lord. This is not a popular message, but it certainly needs to be broadcast far and wide.

Seems to me it might help if I concluded this first chapter with a threefold action plan for making all this happen.

First, to help you cultivate the habit of including the Lord God in every segment of your life, *meet often and alone with Him.*

I freely confess it is easy to slip in this area. We live in busy times. Ours is a fast-paced world. We don't naturally think of meeting often and alone with God; usually we have something else siphoning our time and attention. Nevertheless, I'm still suggesting solitude. It may not be for two hours at a crack. Few of us have that kind of available time in a week, to say nothing of every day. You may have only fifteen minutes to spare and those moments may have to be spent in your car. Quite frankly, you may have to settle for your bathroom.

Wherever, find some place where you can lock yourself in to meet alone with God. You may have to get up a little earlier. Or when life settles down and the dust clears at the end of your day, you may find that late in the evening is the best time for you. Turn the television and the radio off, then in absolute silence talk to Him about this habit of including Him in every segment of your world. Spell out the categories of your life you wish to have Him invade when you're alone with Him.

To make the second suggestion work, that is, refusing to expect or accept any of the glory, *openly admit your struggle with pride*.

If you meet with an accountability group, confess your tendency to seek the glory. It is helpful to tell them. Tell your family. (They're good about reminding you when it resurfaces: "There it is again, Dad.") So, freely admit it. No one has dealt fully with the matter of pride until he or she has first admitted, "I've got a problem with it."

To accomplish the third suggestion—to maintain a top priority relationship with Him—*filter everything through the same question: Will this bring glory to God or to me?* In your mind, ask yourself that question on a regular basis.

Obviously, to ask the question implies that you will answer it honestly. Now I've got good news and bad news. Knowing most of us would rather hear the bad news first, here goes: You can *fake* it! You can actually operate behind an invisible mask and counterfeit this thing called giving glory to God! Most people I know can look back to a time when they faked it. I certainly can! We can look so pious. We can sound so humble.

Eugene Peterson writes:

> Anne Tyler . . . told the story of a middle-aged Baltimore man who passed through people's lives with astonishing aplomb and expertise in assuming roles and gratifying expectations. The novel opens with Morgan watching a puppet show on a church lawn on a Sunday afternoon. A few minutes into the show a young man comes from behind the puppet stage and asks, "Is there a doctor here?" After thirty or forty seconds of silence from the audience, Morgan stands up, slowly and

deliberately approaches the young man and asks, "What is the trouble?" The puppeteer's pregnant wife is in labor; a birth seems imminent. Morgan puts the young couple in the back of his station wagon and sets off for Johns Hopkins Hospital.

Halfway there the husband cries, "The baby is coming!" Morgan, calm and self-assured, pulls to the curb, sends the about-to-be-father to the corner to buy a Sunday paper as a substitute for towels and bed sheets, and delivers the baby. He then drives to the emergency room of the hospital, puts the mother and baby safely on a stretcher, and disappears. After the excitement dies down the couple asks for Dr. Morgan. They want to thank him. No one has ever heard of a Dr. Morgan. They are puzzled—and frustrated that they can't express their gratitude. Several months later they are pushing their baby in a stroller and see Morgan walking on the other side of the street. They run over and greet him, showing him the healthy baby that he brought into the world. They tell him how hard they had looked for him, and of the hospital's bureaucratic incompetence in tracking him down. In an unaccustomed gush of honesty he admits to them that he is not really a doctor. In fact, he runs a hardware store, but they needed a doctor and being a doctor in those circumstances was not all that difficult. It is an image thing, he tells them; you discern what people expect and fit into it. You can get by with it in all the honored professions. Morgan has been doing this all his life, impersonating doctors, lawyers, pastors, and counselors as occasions present themselves. Then he confides, "You know, I would never pretend to be a plumber, or impersonate a butcher—they would find me out in twenty seconds."[7]

Believe me, if Morgan can deliver a baby, you can fake giving God the glory. I plead with you, don't do it! It will come back to haunt you. I know of nothing that makes us feel more hollow or more miserable than playing an inauthentic role behind a mask. Even though you can fake it, don't!

The good news is that you can *make* it. God doesn't mock us. He never gives a goal that we cannot accomplish in His strength. I want to assure you, you can glorify God, you *must* glorify God. But you have to determine deep within your heart that you're going to do it His way. That's right, *His* way.

We've looked at our purpose as the church. And, on a more personal level, we've examined how that purpose can be reality in each of our lives. Let me remind you that, in either case, we stand beside the all-powerful Christ as His Bride and can accomplish sweeping changes in ourselves and our world. Let's do it. And let's never forget it must be done in His strength and for His glory.

1. Take a moment to write down all of your activities and responsibilities associated with the ministry of your local church. Now, as honestly as you are able, between you and the Lord, ask yourself the "Why" question: *Why* are you engaged in each of these endeavors? What are the deep-down reasons? If your prayerful reflection reveals lesser motives than for the glory of your God . . . talk to Him about it. Seek His cleansing and His enabling to reset your sights on the highest purpose of all.

2. What does it mean for you and me to accept (or solicit!) glory which rightfully belongs to the Lord God? What are some subtle ways you might be doing this very thing? Be painfully honest with yourself.

3. Remembering the model of John the Baptizer, determine several practical ways in the next two weeks you could live out the truth of his life goal: "He must increase, but I must decrease." If you have the opportunity, discuss this crucial issue with your spouse or a Christian friend. Throw around some ideas together, and then ask that person to "check in on you" a couple of times to see how you're progressing in your fresh determination to give Him more glory.

OUR OBJECTIVES

Ministry is like mercury . . . it's hard to get a grip on it. And if you mishandle it, people get hurt. Slippery and dangerous, ministry needs to wear a sign like the ones that appear in expensive china shops:

I was looking for a gift in such a shop one Christmas. The place was elegant. Lovely pieces of crystal, exquisite glass statuettes, and a wide assortment of imported china were beautifully displayed on freshly dusted glass shelves. It was one of those impeccable shops where you feel like holding your breath as you glide from aisle to aisle. Your greatest fear is to disturb the delicate balance of a Lladro or inadvertently bump the corner of a shelf holding several Limoges patterns.

Several small signs throughout the shop trumpeted messages like "Fragile!" and "Please Ask for Assistance" and even "Do Not Touch." And there were much larger signs that read "PLEASE TAKE CHILDREN BY THE HAND." The dear woman who ran the place was nervous as a witch in church. She seemed more concerned about protecting her stuff than she was about *selling* it. Every child who entered, even though firmly in the grip of the mother, got a glare from Irritable Irene that would have stopped a clock. I

wondered what she did when we got one of our famous 5.6 earth
tremors. Probably gave up the ghost. I couldn't wait to get out of
there.

It's funny, but most folks don't think of ministry as fragile or
potentially dangerous. Maybe that is why so many are injured by
careless types who push and shove their way through the church,
ignoring the signs and excusing their aggressiveness. The tragic fallout is all around us. Seems a shame that some feel they have a right
to do as they please once the mantle of religious leadership is placed
upon them.

My hope in addressing these things is to increase our awareness
of how God has planned for His church to function—and what we
must do to keep it on course. It is true, the gates of hell will not prevail against it. Clearly, the church is here to stay. But that does not
mean we can do as we please without damage occurring. Open your
eyes and look around. Visit several dozen ministries across the
country. Listen to what is being said or promoted or excused in places
that have forgotten their primary purpose. I ask you, is *that* what God
had in mind when His Son left the earth and delegated the work of
ministry to His band of followers? Is today's concept of the church an
accurate representation of what glorifies His name? I doubt it and so
do you.

TEN STATEMENTS ABOUT THE MINISTRY

While doing my research for this book, I came across a fine, practical volume by a father-son team in ministry, Warren and David
Wiersbe. They have given it an appropriate title, *Making Sense of the
Ministry*. Within those pages are insightful comments that everyone
engaged in ministry should read. I am indebted to the Wiersbes for
the following list, which I have committed to memory. I even suggested that the congregation in Fullerton do the same.

What we have here are ten statements about the ministry that
are essential yet easily forgotten; and when they are, things get out
of whack. Read them slowly and carefully. Think of them as "Handle
with Care" signs.

1. The foundation of ministry is character.

2. The nature of ministry is service.
3. The motive for ministry is love.
4. The measure of ministry is sacrifice.
5. The authority of ministry is submission.
6. The purpose of ministry is the glory of God.
7. The tools of ministry are the Word of God and prayer.
8. The privilege of ministry is growth.
9. The power of ministry is the Holy Spirit.
10. The model for ministry is Jesus Christ.[8]

I rarely make predictions, but here is one I can offer without hesitation. If you will commit that list to memory, review it at least once a month for the rest of your life, and apply it on a regular basis, you will have little trouble staying on target. You will find that many of the things you once worried about or got overly involved in (to the exclusion of the essentials that deserved your time and attention) will quietly fade away. You will also sense a renewal of confidence in your life as you return to things that matter in ministry. In fact, you may find yourself amazed at how brief and simple the number of major objectives there are in ministry. It gets downright exhilarating! Your enthusiasm will return as the load lightens. You may even get excited again. That's okay . . . most of us could use a little excitement. I agree with the late Bishop Handley Moule, who once said, "I'd rather tone down a fanatic than heat up a corpse."[9]

FOUR MAJOR OBJECTIVES AS A CHURCH

At the risk of oversimplification, I suggest there are no less than four major objectives when it comes to the ministry of the church. Whatever we do ought to fall within the parameters of these objectives. I find them woven through the lines of Dr. Luke's words recorded toward the end of the second chapter of Acts.

So then, those who had received his word were baptized; and there were added that day about three thousand souls. And they were continually devoting themselves to the apostles' teaching and to fellowship, to the breaking of bread and to prayer. And everyone kept feeling a sense of awe; and many wonders and signs were

taking place through the apostles. And all those who had believed
were together, and had all things in common; and they began sell-
ing their property and possessions, and were sharing them with all,
as anyone might have need. And day by day continuing with one
mind in the temple, and breaking bread from house to house, they
were taking their meals together with gladness and sincerity of
heart, praising God, and having favor with all the people. And the
Lord was adding to their number day by day those who were being
saved (Acts 2:41–47).

Years ago when our children were small, we subscribed to a
monthly children's magazine. Invariably, soon after its arrival, we
would sit down on the floor at home and find the page that had a
drawing with ten to twelve "hidden pictures" within the one big picture. The children and I would spend the better part of an hour
locating all the little pictures hidden within the larger scene.

As I read this account in Acts 2, I find the church's four major
objectives hidden within the big picture. Speaking of the big picture, it is helpful to understand that this is the earliest moment of
church history on record. Actually, it is the passage of primary reference, since the birthplace of the church is set forth in Acts 2. The
Holy Spirit has come upon those in the Upper Room (Acts 2:1–4)
giving the once-frightened-and-timid men great boldness to declare
the words of life to people in the streets of Jerusalem (vv. 5–13).
Following that, Peter stood and spoke the gospel in a sermon that
was brief yet potent (vv. 14–36), resulting in the salvation of about
three thousand people (vv. 37–41). That is the big picture background to the words we are looking at.

Here were thousands of new believers who had no building in
which to meet, no pastor, no sense of direction, no knowledge of the
Christian life, no church constitution, no set of creeds, no understanding of the Spirit's presence or power, an incomplete Bible . . .
they had nothing! Yet they formed the charter membership of the
church. From this original body of three thousand souls, the flame
spread around the world. And from this original account of their
activities and involvements, we are able to glean the earliest (and

therefore purest) set of objectives. There are four of them.

To keep everything simple and easy to remember, let me suggest the acronym, WIFE.

> W—Worship
> I—Instruction
> F—Fellowship
> E—Expression

As we read verse 42, all four emerge. And then, as we finish the chapter (vv. 43–47), each of the four is illustrated. These major objectives are still relevant, they still comprise the ministry of the church. As we seek to glorify God—our primary purpose—we focus on the fourfold target of worship, instruction, fellowship, and expression.

"W" Represents Worship

Look closer at the Scriptures we just read and observe how the hidden picture of *worship* emerges.

And they were continually devoting themselves to the apostles' teaching and to fellowship, to the breaking of bread and to prayer (v. 42).

When Luke writes that "they were continually devoting themselves," he uses a Greek term that suggests a steadfast, single-minded fidelity. The same original word appears in Acts 1:14 and 6:4, both times referring to prayer. When the early saints met, intensity and full-hearted devotion blended with passionate commitment. Their worship was no halfhearted effort learned by rote. They participated. They got with it!

Verse 42 also mentions their breaking bread and praying together. The immediate result was "everyone kept feeling a sense of awe" (v. 43). Literally, the Greek text says, "And there came to every soul, fear." There was a breath-taking awareness of God's holy presence. A healthy respect for and fear of God pervaded. Was everything somber and morose? No, indeed. We read in this same account of their "gladness," "sincerity" (or simplicity) of heart, and praise of God which resulted in "favor with all the people" (v. 47). The scene is one of spontaneous joy and unrestrained responses of praise.

What fun! How delightful! The Father was being exalted. The Son was lifted up. The Spirit brought fresh expression of freedom. Is there anything more glorious? More pleasurable?

The Lord our God still seeks our worship (John 4:23). He still awaits the praise of His people . . . the wondrous worship of His children. He still longs to inhabit our houses of worship. But, alas, worship is fast becoming a lost art, the missing jewel of this hurried and efficient generation.

In many (most?) churches there are programs and activities . . . but so little worship. There are songs and anthems and musicals . . . but so little worship. There are announcements and readings and prayers . . . but so little worship. The meetings are regular, but dull and predictable. The events are held on time, led by well-meaning people, supported by folks who are faithful and dedicated . . . but that tip-toe expectancy and awe-inspiring delight mixed with a mysterious sense of the fear of almighty God are missing.

Before arguing with me, stop and think. Is *your* church experiencing true worship? Are *you* often near tears or on the edge of ecstasy . . . or so "lost in wonder, love, and praise" that you momentarily forget your whereabouts? Is there really a freedom in your soul, a groundswell of overwhelming gratitude in your spirit, an intensity in prayer that blocks out nonessentials so completely you can concentrate without interruptive thoughts?

Believe me, once you have tasted worship—the kind of worship that captures your heart and rivets your full attention on the living Lord—nothing less satisfies. Nothing else even comes close. Once you have tasted true worship, you will never want to play church again.

"I" REPRESENTS INSTRUCTION

While compiling our list of inspired objectives, we dare not overlook the backbone of the body, *biblical instruction*. The Acts 2 account assures us that the early Christians "were continually devoting themselves to the apostles' teaching" (v. 42). They came to be known as "those who had believed" (v. 44), which implies an objective body of truth mutually embraced. According to Acts 4:4 the church grew as "many of those who had heard the message believed."

Later, as the details of caring for the flock in Jerusalem multiplied, the apostles continued to devote themselves "to prayer and to the ministry of the word" (6:4). No petty concerns, no pressing needs, no priority, not even complaints within the assembly decreased the emphasis on biblical instruction. Nothing caused the leadership in the early church to relinquish the ministry of the Word.

The good news of Jesus Christ's life, death, and resurrection was faithfully declared, so much so that new converts were consistently added to the church. But there was more than the presentation of the gospel. Christians were also fed solid meat and deeper truth from the Scriptures. As the church with all those new Christians grew, there was an increasing need for sound instruction from God's Word.

The same is certainly true today. Often, ministers and churches lose sight of the importance of solid biblical instruction. The gospel is presented, encouragement is provided, events are sponsored, a full calendar of activities is maintained, and the hurting are helped . . . nothing wrong with any of this. But they must not become a replacement for instruction from the Book. Well-fed sheep have a greater tendency to remain healthy sheep. Hungry and emaciated sheep are easy prey to the cults, not to mention their inability to stand up under the numerous battles with life's trials.

Perhaps you are a minister whose responsibilities include the pulpit of a church. Let me reaffirm the importance of your placing a high priority on your time in the study, the cultivation of your skills as an expositor of the Scriptures, and the faithful and frequent declaration of the truth of God. Peter's admonition to "shepherd the flock of God" (1 Peter 5:2) must be understood to include Paul's reminder to "preach the word . . . in season and out of season" (2 Timothy 4:2). Become known as a faithful teacher of the Bible, one who feeds the flock a solid and balanced diet of biblical truth.

Talk about being unique! In this day of shallow sermonettes, syrupy devotionals, and highly emotional tirades that lack scriptural substance, if you prepare and deliver interesting messages that are sourced in Scripture, you will become the talk of the community. More importantly, your flock will become better equipped to assist and serve effectively in the work of ministry. I must warn you, however: Once the sheep have gotten a taste of the good Word of God, they will want more and more . . . so be ready for a lifelong commitment to a strong pulpit. Once our kids got a taste of T-bone steak, they seldom wanted East Texas round steak (hot dogs) again.

Multiple benefits bloom in the soil of this sort of biblical teaching and preaching. A half dozen come to mind. Solid, consistent instruction from God's Word—

- Gives stability to our faith
- Stabilizes us in times of testing
- Enables us to handle the Bible correctly
- Equips us to detect and confront error
- Makes us confident in our walk
- Calms our fears and cancels our superstitions.

I am fully aware that a commitment to instruction can be overemphasized to such an extreme that the church becomes little more than a Bible class. Most of us have seen examples of that, which is why we must not forget that this is one of the church's four major objectives, not the *only* one. A church is to be a learning community along with a worshiping community. To leave out worship and to diminish the outreach and compassion necessary for balance, all the while highlighting only an increased knowledge of the Word, is to buy into an extreme that God never designed for His people. That is instruction gone to seed . . . a heady trip that does little more than puff up pride and turn a congregation into an exclusive club. Let us not only wake up to our objectives, but also be aware of the dangers of becoming out of balance.

Before leaving this objective, it might be helpful to add several ways to know when instruction is moving toward an unhealthy extreme. Three situations bear watching.

First, when knowledge remains theoretical, watch out. It will soon breed indifference or arrogance.

Second, when preaching and teaching are not balanced by love and grace, watch out. Intolerance is not far away.

Third, when teaching becomes an end in itself, watch out. At that point, scriptural instruction is coming dangerously close to bibliolatry.

TWO MORE OBJECTIVES COMPLETE THE PICTURE

I will not try to develop the next two objectives until we get into the next chapter. As you may recall, they are fellowship and expression, representing the horizontal dimension of a church's ministry. The first two (worship and instruction) are more of a vertical nature, entered into in a more individualistic manner. But these last two objectives pull us up close and personal with others. As we shall see in chapter 3, *fellowship* reveals that the church is a *caring* flock. Even in the earliest congregation we find this quality.

> *And all those who had believed were together, and had all things in common; and they began selling their property and possessions, and were sharing them with all, as anyone might have need* (Acts 2:44–45).

> *And the congregation of those who believed were of one heart and soul; and not one of them claimed that anything belonging to him was his own; but all things were common property to them. And with great power the apostles were giving witness to the resurrection of the Lord Jesus, and abundant grace was upon them all. For there was not a needy person among them, for all who were owners of land or houses would sell them and bring the proceeds of the sales, and lay them at the apostles' feet; and they would be distributed to each, as any had need* (Acts 4:32–35).

True fellowship means that we care about and therefore care for one another. And in our *expression* the church reveals that it is a *reaching* body. Expression would include evangelism, a mission vision, reaching out to those outside our circle who are in need, and providing hope and help for those within who require special support. In a word, it is compassion.

Think of it like this: The gospel is like a song. We often give people the *words* and forget they are more attracted to the *tune*. The church gathered and caring for one another is fellowship. The church scattered and reaching out to others is expression. As we shall learn in the next chapter, both are vital.

REASONS WE EMBRACE THESE OBJECTIVES

Take one more look at the last verse in the second chapter of Acts, where we read that the early Christians were

. . . praising God, and having favor with all the people. And the Lord was adding to their number day by day those who were being saved (v. 47).

What a scene! Here in ancient Jerusalem was a group of believers whose worship was spontaneous, whose instruction was substantial, whose fellowship was genuine, and whose expressions were compassionate. No wonder so many new folks were attracted! It is no surprise to me that the Lord added to their number day after day.

When we embrace these objectives, several benefits come our way. Our eyes get off ourselves and onto the Lord. Our own petty differences are minimized, which deepens the unity of the relationships. And all this, when kept in balance, creates such a magnetism that the church becomes irresistible.

And then? Well, then we start becoming what the church was originally designed to be.

It is so easy to lose our way, isn't it? So easy, for example, for a church to become little more than a museum, a dust-collecting group of buildings and pieces of furniture—lots of stuff to look at but lacking dynamic and purpose. Or at the other extreme, it is easy for a church to become nothing but an endless series of activities—lots of motion and noise but very little accomplished of eternal significance.

When the Great Exhibition of the Works of Industry of All Nations was opened by Queen Victoria in 1851, people flocked to Hyde Park to behold what they called the "marvels." The magic power back then was steam . . . steam plows, steam organ, even a steam cannon.

Do you know what won the prize? It was a steam-driven invention that had seven thousand parts—all kinds of pulleys and bells and whistles and gears . . . gears that meshed with other gears that hummed in harmony and whirled in perfect synchronization. It was a sight to behold. Interestingly, it accomplished nothing.

When I heard about that I confess I had this tongue-in-cheek thought: *Sounds like a lot of churches.* All kinds of things are happening, but little is being accomplished. All the more reason to remember our purpose and to carry out our objectives.

The alternative is a high-powered machine that looks impressive and runs on steam . . . which is another word for hot air.

1. Acts 2:42 speaks of an intense devotion to the body of Christ—to the teaching, fellowship, and prayer. This was far more than "habit" or "cultural expectation"—it was a holy passion! How would you characterize your own feelings of devotion and commitment to your local church? If that sense of "steadfast, single-minded fidelity" is lacking, take some time to think and pray the matter through. What do you think diminishes the intensity of your commitment? What might enhance it?

2. Your church may or may not be experiencing the kind of heart-stirring corporate worship I've described in this chapter. For that matter, you may not be in a position to effect or suggest changes in your church's worship service. In any case, you can still take responsibility for your own *personal* worship of God. Take time to jot down some elements of personal worship that need some "exercise" in your life. For instance, how about the place of worshipful music in your heart and home? Why not make it a point to learn a few new praise choruses—or a majestic hymn or two—to sing for your Lord's ears alone? If you can't carry a tune, add a few Christ-honoring recordings to your day—and let your heart sing!

3. To prepare yourself for maximizing corporate worship on Sunday, I suggest you obtain, employ, and enjoy either Karen Mains's helpful volume, *Making Sunday Special* (Word Books), or Anne Ortlund's *Up With Worship* (Gospel Light).

CHAPTER THREE

A GENUINE CONCERN FOR OTHERS

A strange sign appeared on the desk of a Pentagon official. In bold black letters it read:

THE SECRECY OF MY JOB DOES NOT PERMIT ME TO KNOW WHAT I AM DOING

That reminds me of a similar sign that could be placed on many a young minister's desk:

THE SACREDNESS OF MY JOB DOES NOT PERMIT ME TO KNOW WHAT I AM DOING

Such a sign does not actually sit on your minister's desk, but you'd better believe it hangs in many a minister's mind. Many of those serving in local churches and Christian organizations struggle to know exactly what it is they should spend their time doing.

Upon graduation from Bible school or seminary, things seem fairly well-defined. But within a few years so much changes. Expectations intensify. Demands increase. Pressure mounts. Powerful people exert force. His inability to meet every need and fulfill every wish enlarges the tension between the minister and the flock. If the church doesn't grow as rapidly as most had hoped, disappointment mounts. If it does grow, added responsibilities create new complexities nobody expected.

Before long the pastor, whose gift is preaching and whose forte is leadership, is now expected to wear many other hats—construction superintendent, personnel director, organizational wizard, enthusiastic cheerleader, fund raiser, caring visitor, wise counselor, tactful diplomat, zealous evangelist, and a half dozen other roles he never even had to think about back when things were simple and small.

Some who find themselves in ministries that become quite large run for cover and exist in virtual secrecy. It is easier to locate some senators than it is to connect with some high-powered shepherds! As one lady said in an exasperated moment, "My minister is a lot like God—I don't see him all week, and I don't understand him on Sunday!" I find that comment both amusing and revealing. It is interesting to discover how many folks really believe that God is not supposed to be understood; therefore, those who speak for Him represent a rather vague series of responsibilities.

I know that to be the case, having seen the reactions of people through the years who suddenly find out I am in the ministry. A surprised expression is usually followed by a fuzzy remark that reveals a total lack of understanding. I never quite know what to say in return . . . which is why I try my best to keep total strangers from finding out what I do. It is so much easier before the "M" word is used. There is no strain, no awkwardness, not even the slightest feeling of uneasiness between us until the subject of my work surfaces. From then on it is obvious the person doesn't know whether to treat me like a pope or a leper. It's weird!

I could fill a small book with amazing stories of stuff people have done and said shortly after they learned I was in ministry. One fella sitting next to me on a plane during the mealtime nervously changed his request from a Bloody Mary to a ginger ale, whispering to me in a sweat that he really meant to order that in the first place. I told him not to worry . . . I didn't mind at all what he drank, which he thought was a hint, and in a panic he ordered *me* a Bloody Mary. When I declined, he decided to change seats. In his hurry, he spilled his meal all over me. Sometimes it is easier to just tell folks I'm an author. But then they want to know what kind of books I write, and that leads to another Bloody Mary-ginger ale episode.

I will never forget the time I was walking down a long corridor, preparing to make a hospital call. As I approached the parishioner's room, her husband was just leaving. On his way out the door he lit up a cigarette, then glanced down the hall and suddenly recognized me from a distance. I smiled and waved. He nervously waved back and was absolutely at a loss to know how to hide the cigarette from me. Still holding the lighted cigarette, he slid his hand into his pants' pocket! I decided to act as though I hadn't seen it . . . and engage him in a lengthy conversation. It became hilarious. The more we talked the shorter that cigarette got in his hand and the more he looked like a chimney. There was smoke swirling out of his pants' pocket and curling up behind his coat collar. Unable to restrain myself any longer, I asked him why he didn't go ahead and finish his cigarette. Would you believe it? He denied even *having* a cigarette. Within seconds he dashed to the elevator and fled, which is probably good. Had we talked much longer, the poor man would have become a living sacrifice.

Now I ask you, would that have happened had I been an engineer? Or a computer salesman? An airline pilot? Or a librarian? The strange misunderstanding—the foggy thinking—about ministry in general and ministers in particular is astounding.

If I have not clarified it before, let me do so now. There is nothing secret about that which is sacred. The ministry may be an unusual calling, requiring a standard and a commitment greater than others, but there is no reason to perpetuate the erroneous idea that we cannot get a handle on its purpose or understand precisely what it is about. People need to be informed so that the mystery is replaced with reality, which explains why I decided to write this book in the first place. Don't misunderstand. Respect for the ministry is wholesome and needed, but remaining ignorant about it and keeping it in a cloudy fog of superstition or mysticism helps no one.

A BRIEF REVIEW

Even though we have just gotten into the subject, maybe a little review would be helpful. Some of these things we're dealing with are like addition in math. They are so basic, so foundational, we cannot go further until they are firmly in place.

The primary purpose of the church is to glorify God. That, in a nutshell, is the reason we have been left on this planet. We haven't long to live. In our brief span of sixty or seventy years, God graciously allows us breath in our lungs, a heart that beats over a hundred thousand times a day, and sufficient mental and physical strength to carry on. In the process of our earthly existence, His most primary purpose for our lives is not that we make a name for ourselves or accumulate a pile of dough or push people around like a hot shot. Pure and simple, it is to bring glory to His name. If in the process He permits us a measure of success or a few joys and benefits for our labor, no problem. But due to the brevity of life, we must keep first things first.

> The story is told of the man who, while walking on the beach, found washed up on the sand a used magic lamp. When the genie answered his rub, he told him that the lamp contained but one remaining wish. The man pondered for a moment, and then requested a copy of the stock page from the local newspaper, dated exactly one year later. In a puff of smoke, the genie was gone, and in his place was the financial news. Gleefully, the man sat down to peruse his trophy; he could invest with certainty, knowing the winners one year hence. As the paper fell to his lap, it turned over to the obituary column found on the reverse of the page, and the name on the top of the listing caught his attention: it was his![10]

Our God is a jealous God. He shares His glory with no one else. From this day forward, do not allow yourself to forget the importance of glorifying His great name, regardless of your age, your status, your financial portfolio, or your sphere of influence. Read the following reminders of two ancient prophets. They represent words of warning for every generation.

> *Thus says God the* LORD,
> *Who created the heavens and stretched them out,*
> *Who spread out the earth and its offspring,*
> *Who gives breath to the people on it,*
> *And spirit to those who walk in it,*
> *"I am the* LORD, *I have called you in righteousness,*
> *I will also hold you by the hand and watch over you,*
> *And I will appoint you as a covenant to the people,*
> *As a light to the nations,*
> *To open blind eyes,*
> *To bring out prisoners from the dungeon,*
> *And those who dwell in darkness from the prison"* (Isaiah
>   42:5–7).

"'But you, are you seeking great things for yourself? Do not seek them . . .'" (Jeremiah 45:5).

If you're a Bible teacher, you might underline that statement from Jeremiah's pen. If you are a minister, highlight it in yellow. Mark it well. Are you seeking great things for yourself? *Then what in the world are you doing teaching the Bible?* That's God's Book, written for God's glory. Don't seek great things for yourself, regardless of your influence in the ministry.

I'll shoot straight with you, hoping to awaken you to a subtle danger. If your motive is in any way to promote greatness for yourself, you're in the wrong calling. There are no Academy Awards given on earth for people in ministry, nor should there be. Our rewards come later. By His sovereign choice, they come when our King provides them in the future. And it is good to remember that as soon as the crowns are placed on our heads, we will immediately remove them and place them at His feet (where they deserve to be). Why? That's easy to answer: Worthy is the Lamb who was slain, not the one who proclaims the Lamb.

These are not meant to be nice-sounding, soft words of piety. These are true words, easily forgotten, especially if you find yourself in leadership in a growing, dynamic church where God's blessing currently rests. I remind you, such blessing is fragile. It won't last forever.

A CLOSER LOOK AT OUR OBJECTIVES

As we saw in the previous chapter, four major threads are woven into the fabric of Acts 2:41–47. By combining the first letter of each term, the four objectives (Worship, Instruction, Fellowship, and Expression) form the acronym, W-I-F-E.

First, the church is a *worshiping* community. If your church is not engaged in worship, you have to stretch the truth to say it is a church. It may be a fine place to meet. You may enjoy any number of stimulating activities. There may be a lot of great instruction. In fact, that may be the sole emphasis. If so, I suggest that you call it what it is—a school, not a church.

A man told me recently that one of the problems he and his wife encountered in a former church they attended for several years was that the pastor frequently stated, "We don't concern ourselves with a lot of worship here. Music isn't important, neither is fellowship (which he regularly put down). My ministry is teaching . . . just teaching. We get doctrine here."

The man added, "Sure enough, that's exactly what happened. Frankly, it was like attending a Bible school or sitting in a seminary classroom. We even had desks connected to our chairs. After we pledged allegiance to the flag and the minister said a quick prayer, we sat down, and the teaching began. No music. No feeling. No sense of compassion. Boom, we'd open our Bibles and off we'd go!"

Yes, a church *needs* good teaching, but not to the exclusion of worship. I find it interesting that for over three years of ministry on earth, Jesus never told his disciples to write something down.

Not once. His instruction was not an academic exercise. Those who sat at His feet often worshiped, however.

Second, let's remember that the church is a place where we receive *instruction*. We learn from God's Word when we're together, but our learning is not limited to verbal instruction. We learn from the models of one another's lives. We learn from experience. We learn from failure and loss and trials. We learn from the great hymns, from the songs of faith. In the process of learning at the feet of our God, He gets the glory.

You will remember that both of these elements are emphasized in the Acts 2 passage we looked at in the previous chapter.

They were continually devoting themselves to teaching (instruction).

They kept feeling a sense of awe (worship).

When you are in a classroom, you don't feel any awe . . . unless you don't know the answer to a test! That's a different kind of awe. When we truly worship we do so with an awe of wonderment, an awe of praise. There is worship in silence as well—being quiet, being still, knowing that He is God. There is worship in beautiful congregational singing, an anthem, or the wonderful, magnificent music that thunders from a pipe organ.

Once you become aware of worship and instruction in the early church, you realize that both emerge repeatedly through the Book of Acts.

CLOSE FELLOWSHIP

We also find in this same Acts 2 segment that the church is to be a place of *fellowship*. Let's call it a caring flock. The church was never meant to be merely a set of buildings where you come, sit, worship, learn, and leave. The church is a community of believers who demonstrate genuine concern for each other.

The early Christians had a closeness of fellowship rarely found today. They were "continually devoting themselves" to it; not just teaching, not just the Lord's Table and prayer, but also fellowship.

This overused and misunderstood term is from the Greek word *koinonia*, which has the idea of something held in common with others.

When *koinonia* appears in the New Testament, it always has togetherness in mind . . . sharing something together or sharing in something together. The early Christians had things in common with one another. They were together. They didn't come for worship like an isolated bag of marbles that made a lot of noise as they banged together, then marched out in single file. No, they came like a cluster of ripe grapes. As persecution pushed them together, they bled on each other. Their lives naturally ran into each other. How much better it is to think of ourselves as two handfuls of ripe grapes than as a bag of highly polished marbles. Our time together becomes so much more valuable when our lives become entwined with one another, moving closer together, feeling each others' strain and struggles, deeply caring for one another.

One of the root words of *koinonia* takes us to Luke 5:10 where some individuals were called *koinonos*, "business partners." Hebrews 10:33 talks about being sharers and partakers in the gospel. That is from the same root word as found in *koinonia*. Hebrews 13:15 refers to the giving of our money as an expression of *koinonia*. When we truly fellowship, we give; when we give to the needs of an assembly, we participate in fellowship.

Galatians 2:9, it may surprise you, uses the reference "the right hand of fellowship." (You probably thought that expression began in a Southern Baptist Church.) The apostle Paul is describing how willingly they reached out and put their arms around each other. They enfolded themselves in one another's lives.

All this research in Scripture has led me to my own definition of fellowship. Fellowship occurs, I believe, when there are *expressions of genuine Christianity freely shared among God's family members*. I notice from the New Testament that *true koinonia* results in two definite expressions. First, to share something with someone . . . something tangible. To help him meet a need. And second, to share in something *with* someone else. When there is weeping, then you share *in* it with the one who weeps. You also weep. When there is rejoicing, you share *in* the rejoicing with the one who rejoices.

When is the last time one of your peers was promoted and you applauded? Let's imagine a fellow Christian who perhaps hadn't lived as good a Christian life as you; nevertheless, he had recently been blessed of God. Let me ask you directly: Would your thoughts be, "God bless him. I'm thrilled for that family. How happy I am that they can enjoy some of these favors from God"? My wife and I have noticed, quite candidly, that it is easier for more Christians to weep with those who weep than to rejoice with those who rejoice. Somehow, envy or jealousy plays too powerful a role in others' minds when they see someone blessed. Comparison is a nasty game. Let's choose compassion!

Marion Jacobsen, in a book titled *Saints and Snobs*, writes strong but true words:

> If any group of Christians who claims to believe and prac-
> tice all God has said in His Book will face up to their per-
> sonal responsibility within the family of Christ, and to the
> real needs of Christians around them, their church will
> impress its community with the shining goodness of God's
> love—to them AND among them. Such a transformation
> probably would do more to attract others to Jesus Christ
> than any house-to-house canvass, evangelistic campaign
> or new church facility. People are hungry for acceptance,
> love and friends, and unless they find them in the church
> they may not stay there long enough to become personal-
> ly related to Jesus Christ.
>
> People are not persuaded—they're attracted. We must
> be able to communicate far more by what we are than by
> what we say.[11]

TRUE EXPRESSION

The fourth and final distinctive of the church is its *expression*. It is a reaching body. The church is a body that does not keep its hands to itself!

Back in Acts 2:43–46 we found a growing momentum. There was love. There was acceptance. There were vulnerability, compassion, caring, winsomeness, and giving. Needs were obviously being met. In light of all that, we should not be surprised to read how the Lord honored their expressions of concern.

And the Lord was adding to their number day by day those who were being saved (v. 47).

Did the message of the Lord's death and resurrection stay within the church? Did they keep the good news to themselves? Was it something enjoyed only within the walls of their place of worship? No, on the contrary, they couldn't wait to hit the streets and spread the word.

In the very next chapter we read,

Now Peter and John were going up to the temple at the ninth hour . . . (Acts 3:1).

Notice that they were not *in* the temple, they were going *to* the temple. And on their way, at "the hour of prayer," they happened upon a man in need.

And a certain man who had been lame from his mother's womb was being carried along, whom they used to set down every day at the gate of the temple which is called Beautiful, in order to beg alms of those who were entering the temple. And when he saw Peter and John about to go into the temple, he began asking to receive alms (vv. 2–3).

Whenever you travel abroad, you often see similar scenes. People in dire circumstances are quite common in great continents such as Africa and Asia, as well as in sections of the Middle East and South America. Beggars often place themselves near a place of worship. That is where this man was.

Along came Peter and John, whom he addressed, wondering if they would give him something:

And Peter, along with John, fixed his gaze upon him and said, "Look at us!" And he began to give them his attention, expect-

ing to receive something from them. But Peter said, "I do not possess silver and gold, but what I do have I give to you: In the name of Jesus Christ the Nazarene—walk!" And seizing him by the right hand, he raised him up; and immediately his feet and his ankles were strengthened. And with a leap, he stood upright and began to walk; and he entered the temple with them, walking and leaping and praising God (vv. 4–8).

Do you know what then happened after they reached out? They were called on the carpet. By whom? By the *religious* folks, who recited a tired litany of complaints. "We don't have room for this. This is out of the ordinary. Who are you, anyway? You're not one of us, are you?" Instead of being discouraged by the threats from those religious leaders, Peter used the moment as an opportunity to speak up for his Lord.

What a great place to tell people of Christ! There are few places more devoid of spiritual vitality than a religious circle comprised of people who talk about religious things but never mention the Savior. Let's not miss those opportunities. Any time you have a chance to minister to a "religious group," do it. Oftentimes they don't know Christ. They just know about their formal religion.

Back to our story. Thrown back onto the street, guess what? They did the same thing all over again. They are like the child's toy, one of those big vinyl dolls that has a heavy round weight in the bottom. You punch it, it bounces right back up again. Punch it again and back it comes to the upright position. Those early Christians kept coming back up.

Look for yourself—

And as they were speaking to the people, the priests and the captain of the temple guard, and the Sadducees, came upon them, being greatly disturbed because they were teaching the people and proclaiming in Jesus the resurrection from the dead. And they laid hands on them . . . (Acts 4:1–3).

Can't you just hear their captors?
"I thought we told you guys not to do that!"

"Well, we heard you, but we're not going to obey you."
And so they tossed them back in the slammer.

And they laid hands on them, and put them in jail until the next day, for it was already evening. But many of those who had heard the message believed; and the number of the men came to be about five thousand (vv. 3–4).

Remember the figure back in chapter 2? It was "about three thousand." Now it's "about five thousand." The church is growing numerically. Why, of course! Who wouldn't want to be with people this contagious and this courageous?

The beat goes on . . . another you'd-better-knock-it-off scene.

And when they had brought them, they stood them before the Council. And the high priest questioned them, saying, "We gave you strict orders not to continue teaching in this name . . .

(Can't you just see those guys speaking very distinctly through gritted teeth, *"We told you not to do that"?*)

"and behold, you have filled Jerusalem with your teaching, and intend to bring this man's blood upon us." But Peter and the apostles answered and said, "We must obey God rather than men" (5:27–29).

Later Peter preaches to them, and the results were predictable:

But when they heard this, they were cut to the quick and were intending to slay them (v. 33).

Finally, a gentleman named Gamaliel spoke up, "Wait a minute. Hold on, you guys. You gotta realize you may be fighting against God. And if you are, no way can you stop it. And if you're not, it'll stop on its own!" (Swindoll paraphrase). That was Gamaliel's reasoning. Not bad, actually.

So they thought, "Well, okay. We agree with that. But we'll drive the point home. We'll tear the flesh off 'em. That'll remind 'em" (v. 40). Did that stop the disciples' zeal? You gotta be kidding. It poured gasoline on the fire. Those men who were whipped and flogged walked out with bloody clothes, rejoicing that they had been given the privilege of suffering for Christ.

> *So they went on their way from the presence of the Council, rejoicing that they had been considered worthy to suffer shame for His name. And every day, in the temple and from house to house, they kept right on teaching and preaching Jesus as the Christ* (vv. 41–42).

I love it. "Every day" they spoke openly of Christ. Their witnessing wasn't limited to an evangelistic invitation in the church. They modeled true evangelism where the need is—in the street, not the church.

LET'S GET THE WORD OUT!

In my research I have discovered four observations about evangelism and missions in the New Testament.

First: *It was never limited to the church gathering.* In fact, it occurred there least of all. I hope you will remember that. The church gathered is in worship and being instructed. The church scattered is helping and affirming, encouraging and evangelizing. How often I see it reversed! I challenge you to find a place in the New Testament where the church came together strictly for the purpose of evangelism. No, people did not come to church to win the lost. They assembled to worship and be instructed and find close fellowship; they spread out to evangelize. As soon as the meetings were over, they thought about the lost, got in touch with them, connected with them, and won them to the Savior. Once converted, the new believers were brought to the place where they could be instructed, where they could worship, and where they could find genuine compassion, true fellowship.

The church is essentially the place where saints come together to be fed the meat of the Word and to be impressed with the need to share the gospel and its outreaching message. Think of it like a huddle at a football game: You and I know that teams don't show up simply to huddle. They huddle only long enough to know the plays. Through the week we run the plays. Sunday after Sunday we return to the huddle and get the plays.

Second: *Evangelism was always initiated by the Christian*. We have the feeling that if people want to know Christ, they will ask us. We're dreaming if we think folks are going to walk up, tap us on the shoulder, and ask, "Say, could you tell me about knowing Christ as my Savior and Lord?"

In all my years I've seldom had anybody say to me, "You know, I've been concerned about my soul, Chuck. And I know you're a Christian. I'd like you to help me know how to go to heaven."

Are you kidding? They don't bring it up . . . we do. We initiate the contact. Christians did so all the way through the New Testament.

Third: *Evangelism was usually connected with another unrelated event or experience*. I am referring to intense opposition, a healing, a conversation, an argument, a supernatural event, a cataclysmic occurrence. Coming to faith in Christ often grew out of such occurrences.

Fourth: *Evangelism was never something anyone was forced into or manipulated to do*. Scripture contains no record of Christians manipulating unsaved men and women to lead them to salvation. No, almost without exception, people were treated with tact and dignity, with respect and intelligence. Now there certainly was bold conviction, but the early believers gave the message and then waited for the Spirit of God to move. He's never run out of power.

Keep in mind what we learned earlier: The power of the ministry is the Holy Spirit. Caring for people, becoming really interested in their world, their situation, their personal concerns is still the most effective method of winning the lost.

A REALISTIC LOOK AHEAD

I often think of the two dimensions of a church's ministry.

First, *the depth of a church* is determined by its quality of worship and instruction. We cannot give up worship because we believe in evangelism, nor should we. We shouldn't stop instruct-

ing people because we simply love to worship. Having both gives
us depth. The depth of a church is determined by the quality of its
worship and instruction. We must always keep that near the top
level of our awareness.

The second dimension— *the breadth of a church*—is determined by its commitment to fellowship and evangelism. We will
not remain broad if we stop evangelizing (actually, we will become
an exclusive little club). If we forget the world in need, we will not
be a caring flock, we will lack balance. We must keep reaching
out to people who are in need. After all, that is what love is all
about. It is love that pushes us from our smug complacency and
stirs us to reach out and touch others!

> *Love has a hem to her garment*
>   *That trails in the very dust;*
> *It can reach the stains of the streets and the lanes . . .*
> *And because it can, it must.*[12]

It's no secret. The ministry of the church is a genuine concern
for others. We need to stop talking about it and start doing it.

Christ's first order of business is changing the world He died
for. But He doesn't want to turn things around by Himself. He has
asked His Bride to represent Him to the inhabitants of this globe.
Are we ready? He certainly is. And He stands waiting.

1. No matter what the size of your church, it's easy to find your close fellowship limited to the same half-dozen or so people, isn't it? Because it's "comfortable" to be with the same familiar bunch, you may be cutting yourself off from others in the body who could make a real contribution to your life—and you to theirs! I challenge you to invite into your home several couples and/or singles from your fellowship that you don't know very well. Make the time relaxed and informal. Let each person share a little of his or her spiritual pilgrimage—and a few up-to-date concerns or priorities. Just let the conversation flow and watch for opportunities to identify, affirm, and encourage. You will be enriched, and so will your new friends.

2. As we learned in this chapter, *koinonia* also has some financial implications; fellowship and giving are inseparably linked. It may be that you or your family help in the financial support of a certain missionary or Christian worker. Is it simply a matter of writing out a monthly check and sticking it in an envelope? What could you do to draw closer to that individual in a more personal way? In other words, how could you and your family feel more deeply tied to his or her ministry? Are you aware of this person's real challenges and struggles so that you can pray in an informed way? Fellowship is a gift. Make the most of it!

3. Thinking through your present circumstances—your occupation, neighborhood, circle of friends, and so on—what would it mean for you to "take the initiative" to share your faith in Christ? What would be a logical first step? Ask a close Christian friend to

hold you accountable to strategize that first step . . . and do something within the next two weeks. Remember, while some evangelism training is helpful, it is the power of the Spirit unleashed through your fervent prayers that will actually open doors.

CHAPTER FOUR

A CONTAGIOUS STYLE

Y ou can't tell a book by its cover."

It's an old saying but still true. What it looks like on the outside has nothing to do with its content within. The same is true for people. Who hasn't been guilty of jumping to the wrong conclusion about an individual, having formed an opinion strictly on the basis of externals?

What is true of a book or a person is also true of a nation. Popular opinion may prove to be way off target when a serious pursuit of the truth is undertaken.

Take America, for example. We are considered a progressive, culturally refined, and well-educated nation. In comparison to some of the more primitive regions in the world, perhaps we are. But it gets a little embarrassing once you look behind the scenes and tally up the facts.

Dr. George Gallup, responding to the request of the *Dallas Times Herald,* did a survey of students' knowledge in eight industrialized countries. Those currently in school in the United States of America ranked either at the bottom of near the bottom of the list in mathematics, science, and geography. Choosing that latter category, let me give you some glaring examples:

- Only one-fifth of the students being tested could even locate the United States on a map.

- One-third of the teens did not know that Mexico is the country that borders on Texas.

- Twenty-five percent were unaware that New Jersey is on the East Coast and that Oregon is on the West Coast.

- Only about 40 percent could name California as the most populous state.

Gallup found that the aspiring high school graduates who were soon to enter the workplace or university life were woefully ignorant in three major fields: trade, travel, and culture. Their answers to three questions illustrate how true that is.

- What nation in the world has the largest population? The preponderance of the students answered, "The United Nations."

- Which were the last two states admitted into the Union? The majority of answers included Florida, Mexico, and Canada.

- What language is most widely spoken in Latin America? The common response was "Latin."[13]

Not only is it true that you cannot tell a book by its cover or a nation by its reputation, let me assure you of this: *You cannot tell a church by its buildings.* Even though we know that to be true, we still prejudge most churches superficially—and how wrong we often are! For instance . . .

If a church is large, comprised of multiple buildings, "It's a cold church . . . hard to feel close to people . . . they probably don't care that much about others."

If a church is small, out in the country, and nestled in a clump of trees, "It's warm, friendly, and inviting . . . they must have a lot of concern for those who hurt."

If a church is elegant in appearance and made up of affluent, wealthy folks who drive luxury cars, "It can't be all that interested in evangelism or a missionary vision . . . no doubt the pastor is more politician than expositor, probably doesn't really preach the Word."

If a church is simple and plain, "It's gotta be a rigid, intolerant, superlegalistic type place."

If it happens to be a certain denomination, there's an extreme label we tag onto it.

If it is struggling financially, how easy to imagine there has been fiscal irresponsibility.

If it has suffered from a scandal, many would think it lacks convictions and needs a higher standard of holiness.

How erroneous . . . how unfair! What leads us to believe that we can determine the style or convictions or beliefs of a congregation from a quick glance at the architecture of its building or the name of the place?

We need to get beyond the stumbling block of appearances. There is so very little that can be known about the bride on the day she stands before a group of witnesses and well-wishers. And the evaluation we make then can be just as superficial and inaccurate as most of our judgment calls about churches. May God help us conquer the habit of coming to negative conclusions based strictly on a church's size, name, location, or the kinds of cars driven by the people who attend. I would suggest a good place to start would be a careful reading of Matthew 16:15–18 where Jesus made that significant prediction, "I will build My church," followed by a promise that "the gates of Hades shall not overpower it."

Our Lord did not have in mind either a building or a name. Only people. The term "church" comes from the Greek word *eklesia,* meaning "called out ones." Jesus' prediction was that He would reach into the ranks of humanity and "call out" for Himself a people who, by adhering to His teachings, would glorify His name. And His building of that body of believers would be invincible. Not even Satan and his wicked host could thwart the plan.

When did people start thinking of churches in terms of buildings? Are you ready for a shocker? Christians did not begin to erect church buildings until the second century.

VARIOUS "TYPES" OF CHURCHES

Walter Oetting, in his fine little book *The Church of the Catacombs*, writes:

> If you had asked "Where is the church?" in any important city of the ancient world where Christianity had penetrated in the first century, you would have been directed to a group of worshiping people gathered in a house. There was no special building or other tangible wealth with which to associate "church"—only people.[14]

Up through the end of the first century, evangelical congregations met in houses—or wherever they could gather. Sometimes it was in caves and other hidden or underground locations, for fear of being put to death. They never really built church structures that housed worshipers until well into the second century. And it was not until the third century that the emphasis on the structure began to take the place of the emphasis on people.

So down through the centuries, especially in these last two or three centuries, inanimate church buildings have come to represent actual congregations in the minds of the general public . . . which explains why people, when asked the location of a certain church, will invariably refer to a geographical location or a certain architectural design of its buildings.

In fact, there are various kinds or styles of churches referred to these days. One authority has divided churches into four types.

First, he names *the body church*. It is a church that holds no property and needs none. It arranges its worship gatherings according to convenient places to meet. Sometimes, if necessary, quarters will be rented, but never owned. This network of congregational life is most often comprised of small groups, bound together by large-group corporate worship gatherings on a few occasions. But normally it meets in small segments.

A second type of church is what he calls *the cathedral church*. Regardless of its size, this is a church that sees the building as the church. And whatever happens in the name of the church almost without exception happens inside that building or on its campus.

Third, he mentions *the tabernacle church*. This is a congregation of people who have a building, but its building is strictly secondary or functionary. The structure is never considered a holy place in any inherent sense of the word. It is a place that gets people out of the weather, gives them a roof over their heads, and provides a measure of comfort and identity. To them, the facilities serve practical purposes that help in the function of the church. Many things happen in the life of that church outside the building, sometimes many miles removed from its home structure.

The fourth one he mentions is *the phantom church*. This congregation prides itself in having no building of any kind . . . ever. The problem is that it has very little organization of any kind. It is not unlike a Rorschach ink-blot test—each person is able to make of it what he wishes.[15]

Other "church experts" have come up with other possibilities. One such individual is Lyle Schaller, unquestionably one of the most respected authorities on analyzing churches. In his book, *Looking in the Mirror,* he divides churches according to size. He suggests that the smallest church (fewer than 35) is a "cat church." A church of 35 to 100 in number he calls a "collie church." A church of 100 to 175 is a "garden church"; a church of 175 to 225 is a "house church"; and a church of 225 to 450 is a "mansion." If a church has a congregation from 450 to 700, it is a "ranch." Beyond 700 he considers the church a "nation" . . . actually a minidenomination.[16]

My good friend and former senior associate at First Evangelical Free Church, Paul Sailhamer, once came up with another series of groups which made all our pastoral staff smile (he's good at that).

I thought his suggestion was as accurate as anything I'd read or heard.

First of all, there is a *donkey church*. The donkey church is a standard, garden-variety church, regardless of size. It faithfully and relentlessly stays at the task. There is no incredible growth spurt, just a few new folks a year, nothing more. It handles the burdens of ministry like a donkey. It stays at it and gets the job done.

And then there is what Paul calls a *racehorse church*. The racehorse church is a congregation built around only one person. He is clearly the one to put your money on! In brief periods of time there are growth spurts like meteors in the night sky. Zoom—and this year's growth is off last year's graph. The problem is that when the Reverend Hot Dog is gone, the church drops back to where it was before. That's the price the flock pays for depending on him as the racehorse.

Paul then suggests that what we really need to do is to mate a racehorse church with a donkey church . . . and come up with a *mule church*. That's really the kind of church you want to have. Like a mule, it has stability and stick-to-itiveness, but not being all donkey, it also has a great deal of dynamic, somewhat like a fine horse. It has the marks of a racehorse church in that there are individuals within the assembly who give it direction, momentum, charisma, appeal, excitement, and leadership. But, like a donkey, it stays at the task.

But we cannot forget the main drawback . . . to push the analogy a step further. A mule is sterile. It cannot reproduce itself. Maybe that explains an often frustrating phenomenon. When you realize you're a "mule church" with incredible growth, energy, momentum, excitement, and vision, you'd like to start another church just like it. But you can't seem to achieve that same momentum in another location—not even if a few of the main folks are willing to leave and start another church.

The question then is: Why? Why would anyone keep coming to a mule church? Why would it have such magnetism, such solid and consistent growth? Why would it stay so healthy and its people put up with all kinds of difficulties? *What is it that makes it so effective?* It can't be size. It isn't financial wealth. It isn't some supernatural vision unlike any other church. And it certainly isn't limited to a particular personality, because there are often several leaders with persuasive personalities. I can assure you, it isn't convenience! Only the Lord knows how inconvenient it can be to stay involved with a "mule church."

We're back to the bottom line: What is it that makes it work? For lack of a better term, I think it is what I would call a *contagious style*. Even though those words may seem a little superficial, I believe that expression says it best. Some of its success is a bit mysterious. There is an intangible mixture that is downright electric. By the power and permission of the Holy Spirit, the qualities of greatness are present. It's kind of like a lovely moonbeam. You hold it loosely, you enjoy its beauty . . . but you can't control it. You appreciate it, but you know it's bigger than any one person or small group, no matter how influential. It cannot be manipulated or manufactured. It is neither transferable nor easily defined. But when you experience the delight of God's anointing, it is as if you hold your breath and let the wonder in.

WHAT IS MEANT BY A CONTAGIOUS STYLE?

I don't want to leave anyone with merely a vague, misty idea of what I'm describing. So let's turn to an example from the first century, the assembly of believers at Thessalonica. I have in mind the description set forth in the second chapter of 1 Thessalonians.

Since a church is "family," let's think of it as a baby to start with. It has its massive growth spurt in its first year. The first-century church in its growth spurt grew like it will never grow again. Toward the end of that century, the church—the body of Christians—was comprised of people who were turning the world upside down. Who knows? Maybe that will be the last time that will ever be said of the church of Jesus Christ. There is something wonderful about that fresh, innocent era when there was an absence of emphasis on structure and virtually no ecclesiastical politics. There was purity and purging, but through it all there was simplicity. The early church had a style that quickly became so contagious it was not uncommon to find even young Christians willing to die for their faith.

Some of those contagious believers met in Thessalonica.

In the second chapter of his first letter to the Thessalonians, Paul the apostle reflects on his six to eight weeks among them. When you realize that was all the time he was able to invest with the saints in that place, the church seems all the more incredible. While reflecting on his two-month ministry among them, Paul writes:

> *For you yourselves know, brethren, that our coming to you was not in vain* (v. 1).

What a grand memory for Paul, yet rarely claimed by those in ministry today. If I were to engage pastors today in a dialogue, asking them to reflect on former churches they had served, I think many of them would express the feeling that their previous pastorates had been spent in vain. This is perhaps the most common memory a pastor has after having served a church—"So much of it was in vain."

The word *vain* means "empty, unproductive, hollow, lacking in purpose." As Paul looked back to his great days among the Thessalonians, he recalls such dynamic and delight that all feelings of emptiness were removed. "Our coming to you was not in vain." Amazing!

We might be tempted to think he is implying it was easy. On the contrary, the second thing he recalls is what an extremely difficult time it was:

> *But after we had already suffered and been mistreated in Philippi, as you know, we had the boldness in our God to speak to you the gospel of God amid much opposition* (v. 2).

Tough times.

Again, that is not unusual. Anyone who acquaints himself with the details of previous ministries discovers that some of the stronger churches in history triumphantly endured much opposition. Paul came out of Philippi like a wounded rabbit. In spite of mistreatment and opposition, he made his way to Thessalonica. Prior to his two months of ministry there, he had been dumped into prison with Silas at Philippi. At midnight, while the two men were singing hymns to God, there was an earthquake, and they were freed. Finally, they were sent on their way. However, some of the same people who gave Paul grief in Philippi followed, hounding him with the hope of silencing his message at the next stop. To them, Paul was a hated man.

So when he came to Thessalonica, he arrived wounded and bleeding. And when he ministered there, he ministered "amid much opposition." The church at Thessalonica was a young congregation nurtured amidst opposition. Nevertheless, it grew . . . it survived . . . in fact, it flourished!

CHARACTERISTICS OF A CONTAGIOUS STYLE

When you read a little further, you discover some of the reasons the apostle found the Thessalonian church to be a group of Christians with a contagious style. Let me point out a few phrases. Keeping in mind verse 2:

> . . . we had the boldness in our God to speak to you the gospel of God. . . .

Remember his reference to content—the gospel of God.
Verse 4:

> But just as we have been approved by God to be entrusted with the gospel, so we speak, not as pleasing men but God, who examines our hearts.

Verse 8:

> Having thus a fond affection for you, we were well-pleased to impart to you not only the gospel of God but also our own lives, because you had become very dear to us.

Verse 9:

> *For you recall, brethren, our labor and hardship, how working night and day so as not to be a burden to any of you, we proclaimed to you the gospel of God.*

And one more time. Verse 13:

> *And for this reason we also constantly thank God that when you received from us the word of God's message, you accepted it not as the word of men, but for what it really is, the word of God, which also performs its work in you who believe.*

Time and time again, when he reflects on the church at Thessalonica, he calls to mind the substance of his message to the flock.

This brings us to the first of four characteristics of a contagious style. *It is biblical in content.* Were you to have visited among the congregation in ancient Thessalonica, you would surely have heard the clear and consistent declaration of the Word of God.

There are few things more dissatisfying than listening to the idle ramblings of a preacher week after week. Eloquent though he may be, insightful and intelligent as well, a minister with a message based on opinion falls flat when compared to the careful teaching and the faithful applying of the truth of God.

Did you notice how purifying it was? His exhortation did not come from error. Candidly, exhortation will not be in error if the Bible is truly being taught. "Our exhortation did not come from impurity" (God's Word purifies motives and words). Neither did it come "by way of deceit." God's Word cuts the heart out of hypocrisy. It cannot be deceptive and, at the same time, truly biblical.

> *But just as we have been approved by God to be entrusted with the gospel, so we speak, not as pleasing men but God, who examines our hearts* (v. 4).

I love this kind of confident boldness. The more you use Scripture, the less you worry about pleasing the flock. The more you care about presenting what God has said in His Word, the less interested you are in human opinions. A minister who has reverted to flattery has drifted from a proper emphasis on the Scriptures. Show me a pastor who tells the congregation what they *want* to hear and I'll show you a man who has stopped expositing the Book. When you, as a pastor or teacher, commit yourself to the Book, you find that you pay less and less attention to both strokes and attacks from others.

Few people model all this more consistently than British minister John R. W. Stott. In his powerful little book *The Preacher's Portrait*, he addresses the importance of maintaining solid biblical content in our ministry.

> It is not enough for the preacher to know the Word of God: he must know the people to whom he proclaims it. He must not, of course, falsify God's Word in order to make it more appealing. He cannot dilute the strong medicine of Scripture to render it more sweet to the taste. But he may seek to present it to the people in such a way as to commend it to them. For one thing, he will make it simple. . . . The expository preacher is a bridge builder, seeking to span the gulf between the Word of God and the mind of man. He must do his utmost to interpret Scripture so accurately and plainly, and to apply it so forcefully, that the truth crosses the bridge.[17]

A little later he says that the authority of the preacher does not lie in himself, it lies in the Book he proclaims. How often we have heard Billy Graham say, "The Bible says . . . the Bible says . . . the Bible says." All around the world he has been announcing, "The Bible says." And therein is the evangelist's authority.

As Stott says, "In the ideal sermon it is the Word itself which speaks, or rather God in and through His Word. The less the preacher comes between the Word and its hearers, the better."[18]

When you leave after a worship service which has included a significant time of scriptural instruction, you should leave impressed first and foremost with what God has spoken from His

Word, and on the heels of that, with what you must do about it. The varying opinions and vacillating interests of the preacher are secondary to the biblical text. A church that has a contagious style is biblical in content.

It is also *authentic in nature*.

> *For we never came with flattering speech, as you know, nor with a pretext for greed—God is witness—nor did we seek glory from men, either from you or from others, even though as apostles of Christ we might have asserted our authority* (vv. 5–6).

Look back at those two verses very carefully. Read them again. It is clear that the emphasis shifts from the message (vv. 1–4) to the messenger (vv. 5–6). He says, in effect, "My presentation was authentic. I didn't come glad-handing everyone with flattery. I didn't minister with a hidden agenda of greed. I certainly didn't seek glory from the congregation I was serving. Nor did I exploit my privileged position as an apostle of Christ." Those are words of unvarnished authenticity—a true servant's heart. And that kind of authenticity is contagious.

There was no higher authority in the early church than apostolic authority. Apostles had miraculous gifts. They founded churches. They often spoke as the very oracle of God. The New Testament was neither complete nor was it being compiled when Paul ministered in Thessalonica. The only written Scriptures were the Old Testament scrolls. For an apostle to set forth up-to-date, relevant truth from God, he was uniquely inspired so that he spoke *ex cathedra*, declaring without error the very message of God. Such a privileged position was rare and therefore greatly respected. Paul's comment is all the more meaningful in light of this. He refused to take advantage of others or expect penthouse treatment because he filled such an authoritative role in the early church.

While we are on the subject of authenticity, we dare not overlook something he later wrote to the Corinthians. Talk about being real!

> *And when I came to you, brethren, I did not come with supe-*

*riority of speech or of wisdom, proclaiming to you the testimo-
ny of God. For I determined to know nothing among you except
Jesus Christ, and Him crucified. And I was with you in
weakness and in fear and in much trembling. And my message
and my preaching were not in persuasive words of wisdom, but
in demonstration of the Spirit and of power, that your faith
should not rest on the wisdom of men, but on the power of God*
(1 Corinthians 2:1–5).

Authenticity occurs when real people say real things about
real issues with real feelings. There is no phony-baloney going on,
no forked tongue, no religious-sounding words that sound pious
but lack proof. When you're authentic you live what you are. You
say the truth. You admit failure and weakness when it is appropriate. I can assure you, when people discover that a church pro-
motes that kind of authenticity . . . when its leaders model it on a
consistent basis, they cannot stay away. It is like an invisible mag-
net that draws them in.

I saw a small but eloquent sign that had been framed and was
hanging on the wall of a college president's office. It contained
only three words, but, oh, so impressive!

KINDNESS SPOKEN HERE

I'd like to suggest another one for church vestibules and pastor's
studies:

AUTHENTICITY MODELED HERE

A church that consistently remains biblical in content will be
unique. That alone will attract attention. But before long people
who come in will begin to wonder if all this good teaching is just
talk without substance. They will begin to look for authenticity.
Is this a church that really believes what it says it believes? Do we
really carry out what we agreed on in the huddle . . . or do we look
like one team huddling and another running the plays?

The third characteristic of a church with a contagious style: it is a place that is *gracious in attitude*. I love this 1 Thessalonians 2 passage! It drips with graciousness.

> *But we proved to be gentle among you, as a nursing mother tenderly cares for her own children. Having thus a fond affection for you, we were well-pleased to impart to you not only the gospel of God but also our own lives, because you had become very dear to us. For you recall, brethren, our labor and hardship, how working night and day so as not to be a burden to any of you, we proclaimed to you the gospel of God. You are witnesses, and so is God, how devoutly and uprightly and blamelessly we behaved toward you believers; just as you know how we were exhorting and encouraging and imploring each one of you as a father would his own children* (vv. 7–11).

Interesting, isn't it? The opening thought refers to the gentleness of a mother and the closing reference speaks of the leadership of a father. Mark that.

That simple observation tells me the church is a family, not a business. Businesses don't have fathers and mothers; families do. The flock of God is not a corporation gone public. It is open to the public, of course, but the family itself is a unit made up of people who agree on the same basics and find great joy in learning, growing, and sharing in these things. Yet, it isn't uncommon for some in the family to feel uneasy and wrestle with any number of things. They may lack inner peace. The question arises, how do we deal with people who struggle? How are they treated? What kind of spirit pervades? Remember what we just saw? I read *grace* all the way through. I also read *fond affection*. I read of gentleness and encouragement and understanding in Paul's leadership style.

Instead of being harsh and demanding, he was gentle and tolerant. Instead of coming across as a military officer, he came across as a mother tenderly nursing her baby. Instead of shouting strong commands and demanding that everyone fall in line, there was fond affection. In fact, Paul gave not only the gospel, he gave *him-*

self. Instead of seeing the congregation as little more than open mouths needing milk and meat, he said, "You became dear to us." Instead of taking advantage, he said, "I didn't want to be a burden." Instead of engaging in a selfish lifestyle glazed over with a veneer of phony spirituality, he said, "How devoutly and blamelessly we behaved before you, just as a father does before a family he loves."

What a treasure it is to find in the same person a balance of strength and grace. Carl Sandberg, describing Abraham Lincoln, called him "a man of steel and velvet." Sandberg wrote those descriptive words in a speech he delivered on February 12, 1959.

> Not often in the story of mankind does a man arrive on earth who is both steel and velvet, who is as hard as rock and soft as drifting fog, who holds in his heart and mind the paradox of terrible storm and peace unspeakable and perfect . . .

> While the war winds howled, he insisted that the Mississippi was one river meant to belong to one country, that railroad connections from coast to coast must be pushed through . . .

> While the war wavered and broke and came again, as generals failed and campaigns were lost, he held enough forces of the North together to raise new armies and supply them, until generals were found who made war as victorious war has always been made, with terror, frightfulness, destruction . . . valor and sacrifice past words of man to tell . . .

> In the mixed shame and blame of the immense wrongs of two crashing civilizations, often with nothing to say, he said nothing, slept not at all, and on occasions he was seen to weep in a way that made weeping appropriate, decent, majestic.[19]

Steel and velvet. An irresistably contagious combination.

There will be times a church must be steel, and other times it will have to be velvet. A church that is all steel is harsh and calculating and tough. Too much of steel and its message is a tight fist. A church that is all velvet becomes too soft, too tolerant, accepting anything and lacking in conviction. We need both steel and velvet for there to be authenticity, along with grace, truth, and love. How important for a church to stay balanced!

Fourth and finally, a church with a contagious style is *relevant in approach*.

> *. . . So that you may walk in a manner worthy of the God who calls you into His own kingdom and glory. And for this reason we also constantly thank God that when you received from us the word of God's message, you accepted it not as the word of men, but for what it really is, the word of God, which also performs its work in you who believe* (vv. 12–13).

That is a description of relevance in action. Many churches provide what I often call good news for *first-century man*. Yet what we need is good news for *modern man*. We need a message with today's issues in mind. We need application that ties in with today, not the thirties, not the fifties, not even the seventies. Church people need the assurance that the Bible strikes at the heart of today's needs, addressing issues we live with right now.

We don't *make* the Scriptures relevant, they *are* relevant. Our job as Christians is to point out how relevant God's Word really is.

And, by the way, as we embrace an up-to-date relevance, we realize how inaccurate it is to divide things into sacred and secular. Sunday is not sacred, leaving Monday through Saturday in the category of the secular. The way you conduct your business is no less sacred than the way you conduct your worship. Christ and His standard of righteousness penetrate all of life. Each day is equally relevant. God is not out of date.

WHEN THAT STYLE OCCURS . . .

When someone asks, "Say, what kind of church is yours?" Instead of answering "Baptist" or "Presbyterian" or "Charismatic," here is an excellent answer: "We're a church that is biblical in content, authentic in nature, gracious in attitude, and relevant in approach. That's our style. In fact, you'll find us contagious."

When that style occurs, what can we expect?

First, we can expect from God that *He will honor our efforts regardless of our weaknesses.* Second, from ourselves, *we can expect to model first-century Christlikeness in a twentieth-century style.* From others? I think *we can expect them to be a part of the fellowship in spite of the difficulties.*

One of the major secrets to a contagious style is keeping the right perspective. Meaning what? Several contrasts come to my mind.

- More emphasis on content, less on cosmetics

- More importance placed on depth, less on size

- More interest in exalting Christ, less on ourselves

- More reminders that church is people with eternal souls, not structures of tempered steel

- More involvement with the lost outside these walls, not just bringing them in to hear of Christ

- More delight, fewer reminders of duty

- More authenticity, less hypocrisy

- More meaningful relationships, *fewer lengthy meetings.*

Oops—I think I've suddenly stopped writing and started meddling!

1.   Imagine that you, like Paul with the Thessalonians, had only six to eight weeks to touch the lives of the folks in your local fellowship. Knowing that your time was severely limited, what would be the first three to five specific actions you would take to make a difference for Christ within that flock? Knowing that your influence really *is* limited by time (James 4:13–17), which of those actions will you undertake in the Lord's strength within the next month?

2.   Write out 1 Corinthians 2:1–5 on a card and place it somewhere you'll be sure to see the next time you are called upon for any kind of ministry to the body of Christ. Let those words remind you to be *authentic* in your service, neither masking your weaknesses and struggles nor obscuring the truths of Scripture with religious-sounding clichés or self-promotion.

3.   Review again Paul's words in 1 Thessalonians 2:7–11. How was he like a mother with the church? How was he like a father? What are several ways you can apply this tender truth to your own ministry within God's family? Be specific.

CHAPTER FIVE

The Difference Between a Metropolitan and a Neighborhood Mentality

The big church has taken a bum rap.

In this generation especially, size alone makes large places of worship suspect. I find that a rather curious fact since it doesn't seem to be true in other areas of life.

In the domestic realm, for example, big families are not viewed suspiciously. On the contrary, it is usually the large, happy family that is the envy of the neighborhood. You may have a large family and one evening decide to go out to dinner together. There you are, enjoying the time together around the table, and the waiter or someone sitting near you comes over to compliment you. They may even mention how much they admire you. Rather than viewed critically, large families are often envied.

Big is certainly not considered bad in the commercial world. As a matter of fact, every Christmas season I notice that the larger stores and major shopping malls are the most popular places to shop. It is there that we are able to find the gifts we're looking for. Most people seem to think the larger stores and shopping centers have a better selection, are more efficient, and probably offer lower prices than the smaller, privately owned shops.

This is also true of large companies. They are the ones that seem to have the money, the interest, and the personnel to do the kind of research and establish the state-of-the-art standard we have come to expect of quality organizations.

Let me go further. If you need hospital care and have a choice between a large, well-established, up-to-date medical center for help and a much smaller hospital down the street, chances are good you'll go to the larger place because you think you will get better care.

Here's another one. When there is a need for a car, most people don't start with a Sterling or some other lesser-known make. Most people buy one from the "big three" car manufacturers in America or a foreign car made by one of the larger, better-known companies.

This is also true in air travel. Tell me, when was the last time you planned a single-engine flight to Chicago? Unless you own your own plane or have some special, out-of-the-way destination, you and I will travel on a large airliner. And as you are making plans for the flight, you will probably ask, even as I do, what the equipment is going to be. We not only prefer larger planes, we feel a lot safer traveling with the large and well-respected companies.

While I'm at it, how about academic pursuits? I think if we were given a choice in pursuing a higher degree, we probably would not select a school that had twenty-three students with three on the faculty—two of them part-time. No, we would choose one of the larger, respected universities whose degree is admired, whose faculty members often author the textbooks, whose track record is firmly established.

For some reason, this logic breaks down in many people's minds when it comes to churches. Get big and before you know it you're viewed with suspicion, even by fellow Christians. I hope I don't come across as severe or defensive. On more than one occasion back when I was a pastor of a neighborhood church, I used to sigh when some of my Christian friends and fellow ministers would criticize the large downtown church. Some of them felt it was little more than an ego trip for a pulpiteer. Not I. More often than not, I felt the church was another unique witness greatly used of God. I have a host of faults, but for some reason I have never struggled with envy. Because another ministry was big and the place I was serving was small, that never (and I mean *never*) caused me to put down the big church.

But I find that is not true of many Christians. It is not even true of a number of ministers. It may not be true of you, frankly.

What makes me really smile regarding size of church is that the first portrait of the church found in Scripture, the earliest record, mind you, was not your typical "little brown church in the vale." I understand that in order for the earliest church to exist, they had to break up into smaller groups because they simply didn't have buildings in which to meet. There was no such thing as a church staff. They had no church bylaws and constitution. But what makes me smile over this primitive portrait is the enormous size of it. Immediately after Peter preached a dynamic message in the power of the Holy Spirit, God came upon a group of people who were like a mob in the middle of the streets in Jerusalem. According to Acts 2:41, he was the evangelist God used to introduce those people to the good news of Christ. We read they:

> *received his word,* [they] *were baptized.*

This is clearly the first illustration of a group of converted sinners in the era of the New Testament.

> *And there were added that day* [swallow hard] *about three thousand souls.*

Three thousand brand new sinners suddenly came into the family of God. Try to imagine it. Instant growth . . . a church of three thousand. That's enough to make church-growth experts salivate!

But that's not the end, only the beginning. The last verse of Acts 2 says that those people not only related harmoniously, their number grew:

> [They were] *having favor with all the people. And the Lord was adding to their number day by day those who were being saved.*

God didn't come to the place where He said, "Whoops, big enough. In fact, too big. They can't be effective if they grow that rapidly. No church should be that large!" No, indeed. God said, "I will multiply their number."

A short while later, still in the same geographical location, this same body of believers is without a building, without what we would call sufficient staff while the apostles are ministering among them.

> *Many of those who had heard the message believed; and the number of the men came to be about* [gulp!] *five thousand* (Acts 4:4).

You might think because it was in the first century and because God was superintending that work with His great presence, they didn't have the problems people have in churches today. Wrong. Look next at Acts 6:1–4. You wonder if they had our kind of problems? You doubt there were complaints then like there are today? While the church was growing, while the numbers were increasing, while God was blessing and superintending all this—

> *Now at this time while the disciples were increasing in number, a complaint arose on the part of the Hellenistic Jews against the native Hebrews, because their widows were being overlooked in the daily serving of food* (6:1).

I smile when I read those words, not because I am pleased some were being overlooked, but because I understand congregational complaints. Some people in the congregation were probably saying, "It just isn't fair. Obviously those people in leadership aren't concerned. There is a lack of compassion. We need to do something about it. Why don't they get busy and serve these ladies the meals they need? They're hungry!"

The need they were pointing out was legitimate, which the leadership acknowledged. Look at the response:

> And the twelve [that's the staff—the apostles] summoned the congregation of the disciples . . . (6:2a).

I don't know if they called some kind of business meeting or what. (If they did, probably only several hundred showed up. I don't even know where they met!) But they called a group together and said:

> "It is not desirable for us to neglect the word of God in order to serve tables" (v. 2b).

The audacity! I know pastors who have gotten fired for saying things like that. Read on, if you dare:

> "But select from among you, brethren, seven men of good reputation, full of the Spirit and of wisdom, whom we [the Twelve] may put in charge of this task" (v. 3).

You know what their words imply? "We want to meet the needs of those who are not getting fed." And in those days, not getting fed was a matter of daily survival, not just missing a late-night snack. The church helped feed those who were truly hungry. The need was genuine. But the apostles said, in effect, "We're not leaving our top priorities to find recipes, fix meals, clean up the dishes, and serve the hungry. No, you folks need to handle all that. And while you are doing that, we'll stay with the things that are our explicit responsibilities."

> "But we will devote ourselves to prayer, and to the ministry of the word" (6:4).

Remember the list I gave you back in chapter 2? Can you recall the seventh statement on the list? *The tools of ministry are prayer and the Word of God.* Here it is again.

Now let me ask you a very direct question. How open would you have been to the suggestion had the pastoral staff of your church come up with that solution . . . and let's say it was your mother or your widowed sister who was going hungry? I can just imagine the feelings some would have today. They would question the availability, the compassion, even the interest level of the leaders who continued to stay in their cloistered rooms to seek God's face and search the Scriptures for answers and direction.

The point is clear: The apostles' higher priority was maintained. Make no mistake about it, they worked out a way for the needy to be cared for. But they *themselves* stayed with their essential tasks: providing spiritual nourishment so that the saints might take up the work of ministry.

Let me urge you not to be so suspicious of size or to labor under the impression that today's large church is a recent phenomenon brought on by the electronic media. Admittedly, there may be a few exceptions where large churches are little more than studies in religious bureaucracy or where they revolve around an insecure pastor's fragile ego. Yes, those places exist. But through the years God has set apart many larger places of worship and used them effectively.

METROPOLITAN MINISTRIES: NEITHER NEW NOR NOVEL

Let's do a little historical review. For the sake of space and time, I will go back only a couple of centuries and limit my observations to England, then take us across the Atlantic to America. Hopefully, this brief journey into the time tunnel will remind us of the reality that God has blessed and used metropolitan ministries for decades. As we shall see, larger churches should not necessarily be under suspicion as somehow separate from Christ, His Bride, and the plan of redemption.

Carr's Lane Chapel was pastored by a famous man in Birmingham, England. The place was without much appeal, a smoggy, urban ministry, a lot like one would have in downtown New York or Tokyo or Los Angeles today. The man's name was

R. W. Dale. He pastored the church for thirty-six years. It became large and imposing. He was followed by John Henry Jowett, who later came across the Atlantic to the United States and continued to set a new pace in strong expository preaching.

St. Paul's was another large church of renown. It was pastored by the equally famous Henry Liddon, blessed of God as Dale and Jowett had been. In Manchester, Alexander Maclaren spent forty-five years in the large Union Chapel. Alexander Whyte served forty-seven years at the Free St. George's Church in Edinburgh, Scotland . . . another sizable work of God.

We dare not omit Joseph Parker, whose large City Temple was known in London as the public place of worship, second only in size to the famed Metropolitan Tabernacle pastored by the colorful, eloquent—and I might add controversial—Charles Haddon Spurgeon, who at a remarkably young age filled the six-thousand-seat house of worship. One of his biographers states that people waited in the snow for the doors of the Tabernacle to open, so anxious were they to hear him preach. Today, of course, he has been immortalized. But in those days, enormous criticism was leveled against him. Many realized after the fact what a prolific prophet he was. It is amazing what death does to an effective, powerful preacher!

Candidly, I sometimes feel like a maverick in ministry these days. I think I'm a little innovative or creative or "different" . . . then I study some of those greats and realize that by comparison, I'm kind of dull! Spurgeon, for example, was continually criticized for his use of tobacco. He was a cigar smoker. When someone verbally attacked him for that habit, he responded, "If I ever take it to an excess, I will stop." When asked, "What is an excess?" he answered with a twinkle, "Two cigars at once."

G. Campbell Morgan was criticized for his rich taste. It was Morgan, by the way, who ministered for twelve years at the great Westminster Chapel in London . . . and was succeeded by D. Martyn Lloyd-Jones, yet another famous expositor. But it was Morgan who rescued the chapel from decline and dereliction. He was applauded for his insightful expositions, but was criticized for being "extravagant." He said to someone, "I'm not extravagant, I'm just expensive."

Dr. Morgan lived well. He enjoyed nice things, traveled in the finest of coaches, lived in elegant places. And when he spoke outside his own pulpit, he received a large honorarium—something that was criticized in his day. Campbell, by the way, didn't set the figure. An associate in ministry set it for him (maybe he was one of the early agents, I don't know).

In America, we must certainly name George W. Truett, well known for his work at the huge First Baptist Church in downtown Dallas, Texas. He was succeeded by W. A. Criswell, under whose ministry the place has grown even larger. I should also mention Dwight L. Moody who preached to six thousand people at a tabernacle (they called it a "chapel") in Boston.

Boston's Park Street Church was put on the map, in my opinion, by the late Harold J. Ockenga, who preached there for over thirty-two years. At one period of time in his ministry he served as president of Fuller Theological Seminary in Pasadena, California, while he was pastoring Park Street in Boston. Amazing individual.

We cannot omit the famed Moody Memorial Church in Chicago where H. A. Ironside held forth. Or Fourth Memorial Presbyterian Church where Dick Halverson pastored until he became the chaplain of the Senate. And speaking of the chaplain of the Senate, the National Presbyterian Church was a metropolitan ministry blessed of God under the leadership of the late Peter Marshall, whose name and style, to this day, are legendary. And let's not forget Tenth Presbyterian Church in Philadelphia, where the late great Donald Barnhouse ministered so effectively for thirty-three years . . . and now, James Montgomery Boice.

The Church of the Open Door in downtown Los Angeles, another large church, has had several pastors. Perhaps the best-known were R. A. Torrey, Louis T. Talbot, and J. Vernon McGee. What an impact that place has made for the cause of Christ!

Many of my spiritual mentors cut their teeth at the Church of the Open Door while it was located in the heart of Los Angeles near Pershing Square. I should also mention Hollywood Presbyterian Church. There are so many others across the South and Midwest, my list is woefully incomplete. I have not taken the time to include even one of the larger charismatic churches that has been used of God in magnificent ways in this and previous generations, or many of the strong Baptist, Presbyterian, Methodist, or independent ministries across America.

But my point has been made: Metropolitan churches have been on the scene for decades (and will continue to be), and most of them have unquestionably made an impact for good. Nevertheless, in spite of their positive contribution in setting new and innovative trends and attracting many people to join other churches in the same denomination, large churches continue to be viewed negatively, especially in this generation.

It is not simply size that is suspect, often it is rapid growth. When the growth is solid, slow, and steady, nobody gets nervous. When it is sudden and unexpected, all kinds of uneasy feelings occur.

All this reminds me of an analogy we might imagine from a domestic scene. Let's suppose a couple has been married six or seven years, during which time they have no children. Then one day they happily discover they are going to have a baby—a little boy. Lo and behold, a year later they have a little girl. Get the picture? For years they lived together in relative calm and peaceful existence. And then, in what seems like a few months, they're the parents of two busy babies. Things rock along (no pun intended) for four months, then one evening, as they are sitting beside the fireplace, the weary mother says to tired Dad, "Guess what? I'm pregnant. And, honey . . . the doctor says he hears *two* heartbeats." Several months later, twins! And if that's not enough, within a few more months after the birth of the twins, they discover they're going to have triplets.

Whoa! Seven children in an incredibly brief span of time. Believe me, life won't ever be the same in that little condominium with seven kiddos (most of them still in diapers) and all peace and calm gone! How different when it was just Mom and Pop and the stereo softly playing "Sweet Hour of Prayer."

So it is when a church experiences skyrocket growth by God's direction, not the manipulations of some ego-maniac. Question: What do you do? How do you handle it? What are the principles necessary for keeping it effective? Let's get painfully practical.

Timeless Principles for Staying Effective

Back in the Old Testament, we have a wonderful portrait of a man I'm going to call the senior pastor of the Wilderness Bible Church. His name is Moses. What an unusual minister! You would never have chosen him had you sat in on the candidating committee looking for the pastor of this unusual "church." For starters, the place he will minister is an unusual church because of its size—about two million, give or take a few thousand. Furthermore, his background is questionable. He killed a man. Nor has this gentleman set many impressive records in the last forty years of his life—which brings us to his age. He's now *eighty*, not the ideal age for a man who must shepherd so many people with no staff. And no building!

For the last four decades he has worked for his father-in-law Jethro leading sheep, which is about the only thing we could point to that has remotely prepared him for this vast congregation. And did I mention his speech impediment? Along with old age and a bad résumé working against him, the man *stutters*. Dear Moses . . . what a challenge!

Without warning, a bush bursts into flame and refuses to quit burning. The eighty-year-old shepherd stares in disbelief until he hears his name being called. Understand, he hadn't the foggiest notion he would ever be called back into God's plan of action. He has been crushed to nothing. So he has nothing but character to offer. I still don't think we would have been that impressed with him. Contrary to popular twentieth-century opinion, he did not look like Charlton Heston—nor did he have the physique of Rambo. Moses, plain and simple, was a broken octogenarian who didn't want the job. Reluctantly, after a lengthy argument, he finally takes it. Virtually overnight, he becomes the "pastor" of two million cantankerous souls recently released from slavery.

The story I have in mind begins with a visit. To stay with my analogy, this aging senior pastor spends some time with a consultant named Jethro, who happened to be his father-in-law. It's a pleasant encounter, full of warm hospitality. Exodus 18 records the scene:

> And Moses told his father-in-law all that the LORD had done to Pharaoh and to the Egyptians for Israel's sake, all the hardship that had befallen them on the journey, and how the LORD had delivered them (v. 8).

Can't you just hear the excitement? "Let me tell what God has done. Listen, Jethro, you wouldn't believe the whole Red Sea thing. Amazing, I still can hardly believe it! I just said, 'Stand still and watch the deliverance of the Lord,' and whoosh! the waters rolled back, the sea bed dried up, and we *walked* through it. Suddenly, as we all looked back, the Egyptians were destroyed!"

Jethro is stroking his beard, saying, "Wow! I believe it. It is incredible."

> And Jethro rejoiced over all the goodness which the LORD had done to Israel, in delivering them from the hand of the Egyptians. So Jethro said, "Blessed be the LORD who delivered you from the hand of the Egyptians and from the hand of Pharaoh, and who delivered the people from under the hand of the Egyptians. Now I know that the LORD is greater than all the gods; indeed, it was proven when they dealt proudly against the people." Then Jethro, Moses' father-in-law, took a burnt offering and sacrifices for God, and Aaron came with all the elders of Israel to eat a meal with Moses' father-in-law before God (vv. 9–12).

As the day ended, they enjoyed a closeness of fellowship together. The night brought both of them much-needed rest. The following day, however, things changed.

And it came about the next day that Moses sat to judge the people, and the people stood about Moses from the morning until the evening. Now when Moses' father-in-law saw all that he was doing for the people, he said, "What is this thing that you are doing for the people? Why do you alone sit as judge and all the people stand about you from morning until evening?" (vv. 13–14).

Like a good consultant, Jethro doesn't immediately give answers, he asks questions: "What is going on? Why are you doing all this alone?" I hope you have that word circled in your Bible—*alone*. It is important.

Now look at Moses' humble and sincere answer:

And Moses said to his father-in-law, "Because the people come to me to inquire of God" (v. 15).

"That's my job, man. I mean, how can I have the right to commune with my Lord at the end of a day and say, 'I ministered in Your name,' if I don't help all the people with all their needs?"

Don't criticize Moses. He just doesn't know any better. He's doing what he has always done. It is a "neighborhood" organization style of leadership, still common in most ministries today—even in large churches. It never dawned on Moses to do something about the workload. Delegation was not a word in his vocabulary.

And Moses' father-in-law said to him, "The thing that you are doing is not good."

(The Hebrew sentence is even stronger. It begins *"Not good!"* Literally, "Not good is this thing you're doing!")

"You will surely wear out, both yourself and these people who

are with you, for the task is too heavy for you; you cannot do it alone" (v. 17–18).

The Hebrew terms translated "You will surely wear out" convey the idea of becoming old and exhausted. Today, we would say, "You know, Son, if you keep this up, you'll die an early death. You're only eighty(!). You have lots of good years in front of you."

Don't miss something else in Jethro's honest reproof; it's exhausting for *the people,* too. They will get worn out waiting for Moses to help them.

How many pastors, how many administrators, how many presidents of schools, how many fine Christian men and women, CEOs of religious organizations, and church leaders are trying to do it all alone? More than we'd ever believe! And to make matters worse, the congregations and related staffs are letting them do it! By the way, much of this applies just as directly to a church of two hundred as it does to a church of two thousand.

I like the way Jethro takes charge. "Now you listen to me." That's the next verse (sounds like a father-in-law, doesn't it?). Jethro doesn't throw rocks at Moses and watch him bleed. He offers wise, workable counsel.

> *"Now listen to me: I shall give you counsel, and God be with you. You be the people's representative before God, and you bring the disputes to God"* (v. 19).

I love that. I'm not suggesting that you kick back, play golf four days a week, put everything on hold, and hide out until late Saturday night. The hope for the senior minister is not that he becomes so far removed he doesn't know what's going on. No, what he must come to terms with is the issue of *priorities.*

Jethro says, "You represent the needs of the people to the living God." He doesn't stop there, however.

> *"Then teach them the statutes and the laws, and make known to them the way in which they are to walk, and the work they are to do"* (v. 20).

"Tell them, Moses. Teach them. Make truth known to them. And when you've done it, teach them more and more and more." In fact, the last Book of the Law, which Moses wrote, is nothing but teaching . . . sermon after sermon. It is named Deuteronomy (meaning "a repetition of the Law"). He goes over and over the same ground. He is teaching the people, as Jethro urged him to do.

When a leader (including a pastor) gets too detailed in the nuts and bolts of the organization, he stops communicating. You may be a minister and find yourself in that predicament right now. You're involved. You know all the details—too many, in fact. You are well-acquainted with everybody's complaint. You mentally rehearse all their expectations. The result is tragic! Your leadership is now reduced to handling all the switches, gears, and pulleys. You're the answer man, the errand boy, the congregation's slave. But the problem is, you're not really *leading*. If the truth were known, you haven't had a creative idea in months. You've even stopped dreaming. Your world is made up of putting out fires. You've become a manager of details, but not much of a leader.

According to an article in a recent issue of the *Wall Street Journal*, when Benno Schmidt, Jr. assumed the presidency of Yale University, he expressed some fear regarding the busyness of the job. He said, "If I can't put my feet on the desk and look out the window and think without an agenda, I may be *managing* Yale, but I won't be *leading* it."

That is an insightful (and I might add convicting) comment every minister should remember. Managing is one thing, leading another. Churches need leaders!

"Moses, you have to get with God. You have to hear God's voice and communicate His truth. Even if some beg for time with you, just say 'No!' Say it until they understand it is going to be delegated to people just as qualified who happen to have similar gifts, more time, and sufficient abilities—even more than you. Say 'No' more and more, Moses! Leaders who don't know how to say 'No' lose their effectiveness."

Plan "A" is *communication*. It is written between the lines: "Instruct the people in the truth of God. That's essential. Don't be reluctant about it. Do it, Moses. Do it with all your heart."

But that was not all.

> *"Furthermore, you shall select out of all the people able men who fear God, men of truth, those who hate dishonest gain; and you shall place these over them, as leaders of thousands, of hundreds, of fifties and of tens"* (v. 21).

Plan "B" is *delegation*. Pass the workload around, but not just to any Tom, Dick, and Harry. Find quality people who can handle a thousand—give them the larger group. Find those who can lead hundreds—give them a smaller group. Find those who can lead groups of fifty and give them that number. Find those who can handle ten and give them the smallest size group. Let them all invest their gifts, time, energy, and wisdom with those groups. Let 'em do it . . . don't step in and do it for them!

> *"And let them judge the people at all times; and let it be that every major dispute they will bring to you . . ."* (v. 22).

Even as I write this sentence I know that this becomes subjective. We have no detailed list here (or anywhere else in Scripture) as to what constitutes a "major" or "minor" dispute. That has to be hammered out. To come to terms with these differences takes wisdom, time, and discussion. It also requires trial-and-error experience. That is why Scripture warns us against having a novice as a pastor of a church. One of the assignments of a seasoned man is the ability to determine major from minor, to know when it is best to say "Yes" and when he must say "No," even when it is unpopular. Church boards need to assist a pastor in working through these details.

Are you ready for a shocker? Read this very slowly:

> *"And let them judge the people at all times; and let it be that every major dispute they will bring to you, but every minor dis-*

pute they themselves will judge. So it will be easier for you, and they will bear the burden with you" (v. 22).

Did you catch that? "So it will be easier for you. . . ." I have never once heard that sufficiently emphasized at a pastors' conference. No seminar is ever titled: "How to Make the Ministry Easier," or "How to Have the Time of Your Life." No, at those highly intensified settings, you're supposed to help pastors know how to do more and more—until they slump under an increasing load of guilt.

You've seen the humble, overworked, underpaid pastoral slump, haven't you? It's pathetic! It looks like somebody has hit the guy with a big two-by-four across the back of his head. He's kind of bent forward, looking down, and appears sad and somber, seldom smiling . . . never laughing. In case you haven't heard, that is what you're supposed to look like if you're really dedicated to the ministry. I've got a great Hebrew word for that nonsense: *Hogwash!*

According to Exodus 18:22, if we communicate and delegate, it is supposed to get *easier* for us, because others are involved in bearing the burden with us. Yes, *easier*.

It has always bothered me that it is not considered very spiritual if you're in the ministry yet having a lot of fun. I have a question for all who believe that: Since when is exhaustion the proof of efficiency? Here's another one not nearly so nice: Who says that winding up in a mental hospital, emotionally spent and physically exhausted, is proof that the pastor really gave it his best? I have a big bone to pick with those who took the fun out of ministry and turned serving into slavery. Who stole the laughter from the pastor's home or took the joy from his study? Who robbed the pastor's wife of the freedom to enjoy her role and to be herself? Cursed thief!

There is enough potential stress in most churches to exhaust ten pastors if we allow it. But God's desire is that we find ways to make it "easier."

"If you do this thing and God so commands you, then you will

be able to endure, and all these people also will go to their place in peace" (v. 23).

What wise counsel! Thanks, Jethro. And the good news is that Moses took his father-in-law's advice . . . and it worked beautifully. Pastor Moses lived to be 120 years old. And when he died, Scripture says he was the meekest man on the face of the earth. I don't think there was a bitter bone in his body. He learned to live free of needless burdens. So can you, my friend. In summary:

- Your ministry will become easier for you.

- Others will feel a significant part of the work.

- You will live happier and longer.

- It will work!

HOW DOES ALL THIS APPLY TO A METROPOLITAN MINISTRY?

You are probably wondering how all this applies to you personally—to your ministry or the ministry of your church. Let's see if I can clarify the application by listing three thoughts I frequently review. They help me maintain perspective.

1. Many people, plus high expectations, multiplied by numerous needs, equal endless responsibilities.

2. As work increases, the load must be shifted. (Efficiency sometimes reveals itself not by what one accomplishes but by what one *relinquishes*.)

3. God's personal servants are not exempt from the penalties of breaking God's natural laws. Not enough sleep means illness. Not enough relaxation means anxiety. Trust me, there is nothing spiritual about a bleeding ulcer. A man is of no use flat on his back, broken, and struggling with bitterness. Pastors can crack up. So can pastors' wives. Pastors can lose their families, wives, and children. Pastors can die young.

Every ministry that hopes to continue on the cutting edge must come back to an evaluation of where it is going and what it hopes to accomplish. Is the load being sufficiently shifted? If not, let's keep shifting it or we will lose our best people, lay and clergy alike.

Ephesians 4 gives some great encouragement for shifting the load to gifted people within the body. It includes the titles of several spiritual gifts. These gifts, as they are at work in the church, allow the work to get done smoothly and efficiently.

> *And He gave some as apostles, and some as prophets, and some as evangelists, and some as pastors and teachers . . .* (Ephesians 4:11).

This list is a limited representation of all the gifts in the body. Other gifts worthy of your attention are listed in Romans 12, 1 Corinthians 12, and 1 Peter 4. Study the lists. There are helpers. There are people who organize. There are people with mercy and counseling gifts. There are people with wisdom and utterance gifts (we often refer to them as teachers). Not all teachers are pastors, but all pastors are to be teachers. That is not a tongue twister. One can teach a class, but not have the gift of pastoring. But if one accepts the role of pastor, he must have the gift of teaching as well. There are other gifts: evangelism, giving, exhortation, and any number of other abilities. Wise is the minister who teaches his flock about spiritual gifts, explaining the value of each, then encourages them to function so he can maintain his emphasis on prayer and the ministry of the Word.

I find at least three principles in the Ephesians 4 passage. First, *there are sufficient gifts to sustain any size church.* God gave His family gifts

> *for the equipping of the saints for the work of service, to the building up of the body of Christ* (v. 12).

Let me address you who are ministers. If you happen to be in a church that, in spite of your efforts to delegate the workload, is not sustaining itself with the gifts within it, then may I be so bold as to suggest that you deliberately teach on spiritual gifts. Willingly delegate the workload. If you find the board and flock unwilling to share the responsibilities of ministry, perhaps you should consider moving on to a ministry that allows such gifts to function. I'm of the opinion, though it may sound like heresy, that some smaller churches constantly struggling to exist ought to be shut down—or merged so that they might survive, thrive, and get a quality job done. One exhausted man's struggle to keep everything afloat is not a church, it is a tragic study in unbiblical futility.

All this brings me to a second principle: *When the gifts are exercised, congregations grow up.*

> *Until we all attain to the unity of the faith, and of the knowledge of the Son of God, to a mature man, to the measure of the stature which belongs to the fulness of Christ. As a result, we are no longer to be children, tossed here and there by waves, and carried about by every wind of doctrine, by the trickery of men, by craftiness in deceitful scheming* (vv. 13–14).

Believers need to be in the Lord's service because we are all engaged in ministry. Each Christian should be involved in the exercise of his or her spiritual gift. The work of the church is a mutual ministry. As we exercise our gift(s), we mature. And, I repeat, the joy returns as the ministry becomes easier.

The third principle is, *maximum involvement leads to healthy growth.*

> *As a result, we are no longer to be children, tossed here and there by waves, and carried about by every wind of doctrine, by the trickery of men, by craftiness in deceitful scheming; but speaking the truth in love, we are to grow up in all aspects into Him, who is the head, even Christ, from whom the whole body, being fitted and held together by that which every joint supplies, according to the proper working of each individual part, causes the growth of the body for the building up of itself in love* (v. 14–16).

Serving the Lord causes healthy spiritual growth. When it takes place, few things are more exciting or more impressive.

Years ago I created a chart that grew out of many years' experience in ministry. I have placed it on the following page. It states, rather simply, two contrasting philosophies—the "neighborhood" mentality and the "metropolitan" mentality. Not until we wake up to and accept the differences between these two concepts will we come to terms with many of the frustrations that plague most churches. On the left you will see a listing of that which characterizes the small-church mentality. And by the way, I've seen large churches still operating under a "neighborhood" concept. On the right side you will see the "metropolitan" concept, which I think is what makes life possible in a large church. Pause a few moments and study the chart.

Neighborhood Mentality

Even though much of the chart is self-explanatory, perhaps a few comments will help. In the "neighborhood" concept, there are close ties between pastor and people—the church is like one big family. Everybody identifies with the pastor. When he is there, "the show goes on." When he is not there, the lights are out. Why? Because the pastor is the center of whatever is happening.

There is also the smaller scale everyone needs to accept. Everything is smaller—staff, vision, organization, and facilities. The budget is downscale and simple. The outreach is also small. Provisions are small, and the variety is small.

When it comes to geography, the congregation is drawn mainly from a close radius. I would imagine when our church began, we drew our congregation from just a few miles around. I doubt that anyone drove from Pasadena, Long Beach, or Newport Beach, as they do now. I met a couple last Sunday who drives from San Bernardino every Lord's Day. They travel an hour or so to worship with us (I encouraged them not to, but they said they choose to do that).

I would imagine some people in Spurgeon's day traveled across London to attend the Tabernacle. I know I would have. Some of you would have, as well.

THE "NEIGHBORHOOD" CONCEPT	THE "METROPOLITAN" CONCEPT
1. Close ties between pastor and people—"one big family . . . identifies with the pastor"	1. Close ties between identity groups—"numerous families . . . identify with one another"
2. Smaller scale: staff . . . vision . . . organization . . . facilities . . . budget . . . outreach . . . provision . . . variety	2. Large scale: staff . . . vision . . . organization . . . facilities . . . budget . . . outreach . . . provision . . . variety
3. Congregation drawn mainly from *close* radius	3. Congregation drawn from *vast* radius
4. Tendency to be "inbred" . . . narrow rotation among lay leadership . . . greater reticence to change	4. Less "inbred" . . . broad rotation among lay leadership . . . less reticence to change
5. Easy to know everyone	5. Impossible to know everyone
6. Workload borne by volunteers	6. Some work delegated to specialists
7. Relatively simple to manage and maintain	7. Complex to manage and maintain
8. One-man operation . . . more rigid control	8. Multi-staff . . . team emphasis among all in leadership . . . broader base of control
9. Strong, centralized loyalty to "the church" . . . easier to implement involvement	9. Loyalty decentralized to various ministries . . . more difficult to implement involvement
10. Atmosphere naturally warm and friendly	10. Atmosphere can still be warm and friendly—but a constant challenge

There is the tendency to be "inbred" in the smaller church. There's a tight, narrow rotation among the lay leadership. The same group of officers return to be elected on a regular basis. There is also a greater reticence to change than in a metropolitan ministry. Traditionalism runs deep.

It is easy to know everybody. You know when somebody goes to the hospital. You know when a mother has a baby . . . you even know what they named the baby. A wedding is equally significant. In metropolitan ministries, however, there may be two to three weddings on a weekend, and only those in each couple's circle of friends would know about it.

The neighborhood concept is relatively simple to manage and maintain. It's a one-man operation. Take that literally. The pastor carries the key to the church. He is often the one who draws the water before a baptism. He has a key for the fellowship hall and is involved in the church suppers. He also carries the key to the thermostat so he personally can determine the building's temperature. If the little church is heated by a wood stove, he stokes it every Sunday morning nice and early and has the building warm when people arrive.

So goes life in a little neighborhood church. Sounds like shades of Lake Wobegon, doesn't it? If that's your preference, it's wonderful. It is the style or philosophy that fits a neighborhood church. It works in a small, neighborhood ministry. But in a church of a thousand or more you cannot carry enough keys. Or enough salad. Or enough wood. You can't keep up.

In a smaller ministry where everyone knows each other, it is easier to implement involvement. The atmosphere is naturally warm and friendly.

Metropolitan Mentality

Moving to the other side of the chart, we immediately see the series of contrasting realities. There are close ties but they are between identity groups. You find your close ties in the adult fellowship you attend. You may sing in the choir, so that group becomes your flock. Maybe you are on the trustee board and that's your identity group. Maybe you're on the pastoral staff and that's your group. Or maybe you're a shepherd of a smaller cell group that meets as a Bible study on Thursday evenings. That group becomes your point of reference, your place of identity.

Everything is on a larger scale: larger staff, larger vision, larger organization, larger facilities, larger budget, and larger provisions.

In a metropolitan ministry as I described earlier, the flock is drawn from a vast radius. You will meet people from all over. You will draw visitors from around the country. All of this fits the scheme of things. You cannot fight it. It is going to happen.

Furthermore, it is less inbred. The rotation among the lay leadership means you will know fewer of those officers personally. In a larger ministry, there is less traditionalism, less reticence to change. (Notice I didn't say "no" reticence to change, I said "less.")

It is impossible to know everyone. Much of the hands-on work has to be delegated to specialists. Many of them are paid. It is complex to manage and maintain. This is no one-man operation; there is a multiple staff. Loyalty is decentralized to various ministries. And let me put your mind at ease . . . the atmosphere can be warm and friendly, but it is a *constant challenge*.

I distinctly remember coming to First Evangelical Free Church way back in 1971 and wanting to get my arms around all the people who were attending on Sundays, some eight hundred or nine hundred people. I had come from a church in Texas that was almost the same size and had started as a neighborhood ministry. And the church I pastored before that in Massachusetts was also a neighborhood ministry. Naturally, I wanted to stretch my arms around everybody.

I kept trying to remember everyone's name, and I couldn't do it. I still remember thinking, "I'm trying, but I can't eat this elephant. I'm doing good just to hang on to the tail of this thing." I soon realized I needed both a qualified staff and an involved congregation to help take up the work of the ministry. I remember saying quite often, "That is the only way we are going to survive."

Why did I stay at the same church for well over twenty years? Because the flock was willing to leave all those dreamy "neighborhood" ideals and live with the reality that we were unquestionably a metropolitan ministry. When complaints arose, they were from those in the flock who still hung on to their "neighborhood" expectations.

Admittedly in a large church the responsibilities are numerous and the expectations can be staggering. But it is exactly where I wanted to be. It is where I was called. I loved the staff, the harmony, and the direction we were going. Every once in a while I had to take a deep breath and tell myself that it was okay that I wasn't touching all the bases. I couldn't even find some of them! Someone could, though. It was tough being a people-person and not being able to recall that husband's name or know how many kids another couple had. I loved being personally involved, but it was not possible after a certain point.

Let me repeat something for the sake of emphasis. Those who were frustrated at the Fullerton church were usually those who embraced a neighborhood mentality. My counsel to them from time to time was, "Find a *neighborhood* church . . . for your sake, for your family's sake—and for *our* sake!" They usually took my advice, and everyone was relieved!

All "neighborhood" folks need to find a place that's a size they can get their arms around so they can feel fulfilled. I write that with only the right spirit. I have said it from the pulpit, so I might as well write it in a book. A metropolitan church will only frustrate those who long for a neighborhood ministry. Candidly, the sooner they make a change, the happier everyone will be. That's not a subtle threat, it's a sincere promise.

KEEP THESE THINGS IN MIND

This fifth chapter has become much longer than I had originally planned. We have covered a lot of territory, however, and every step of the way has been valuable.

Let me suggest three practical things for you to keep in mind as you wake up to the difference between a "neighborhood" mentality and a "metropolitan" mentality. I hope this summary will rivet what we have discovered into our heads. If you are in the process of shifting, you need to cling to these three reminders.

First, *if you have neighborhood expectations you will be frustrated in a metropolitan church.* The reverse is equally true. Such things as regular and intimate ties with the senior pastor or immediate attention from him when you need someone to talk to or being known by name among those sitting around you in worship—these are all unrealistic expectations in metropolitan ministries.

Second, *broad-minded flexibility and small-group participation are major secrets of survival for a healthy metropolitan church.* Don't expect a special parking slot or the same spot on the same pew every Sunday. Be thankful you found a place—any place! Stay open to a variety of musical selections and styles. Get involved in a small group. Think of yourself as a minister, touching others' lives.

Third, *changing methods doesn't mean a changing message.*

No need to develop that any further here . . . it's the subject of my next chapter. Stay tuned.

1. Even though you may not be on the pastoral staff of your church, you are still called to be a "minister." Ponder the listings of gifts in Ephesians 4, Romans 12, 1 Corinthians 12, and 1 Peter 4. (It might be helpful to reread those passages in a paraphrase, such as *The Living Bible* or J. B. Phillips's *New Testament in Modern English*.) Do you see yourself, your God-given strengths and bents, in any of these Scriptures? If you've been waiting around for your gift to be revealed in a blaze of light from heaven—you've been waiting too long! If a particular service niche hasn't become obvious to you, plunge into the work where you see need. Sometimes the only way we'll ever discover our gifts is by trying different things. Remember, God doesn't expect perfection, just a willing heart and hands.

2. Are you in an area where a "neighborhood" church is the only viable option? What positive principles from the "metropolitan" ministry might be implemented in a smaller-scale work?

3. Are you in a "metropolitan" church feeling frustrated and somewhat lost by the bigness of it all? Don't allow that frustration to hold you in an unhappy, no-growth mode for precious weeks, months, and years. Take the time to consider where you could fit in as a member of a smaller group within the body. Yes, it will take initiative, and yes, it is difficult at times to "break in" to a group of folks you don't know well. But the other members of the body need you, just as you need them, to live a fulfilled, productive Christian life. Ask for God's help, swallow hard, and take that first step! Be open to the fact that He may be leading you to another church . . . one where you feel much more comfortable with its philosophy.

WHAT CHANGES AND WHAT DOESN'T

The good ol' days."

Virtually every week of my life I come across folks who long for those times. I often wonder what they have in mind.

I think they mean back when haircuts cost "two bits" and watching the Brooklyn Dodgers cost "four bits." They visualize some kind of golden, idyllic existence: no energy crisis, clean air, clear rivers and streams, close families, fun at school . . . you know, the simple life. Today, if you pick up the newspaper, turn to a scandal section or the editorial page, and read of a hectic lifestyle, violence in the streets, and high-pressured politics, the tendency is to sigh and wish for days past.

Here's an example from a national periodical:

The world is too big for us. Too much going on, too many crimes, too much violence and excitement. Try as you will, you get behind in the race, in spite of yourself. It's an incessant strain, to keep pace . . . and still, you lose ground. Science empties its discoveries on you so fast that you stagger beneath them in hopeless bewilderment. The political world is news seen so rapidly, you're out of breath trying to keep pace with who's in and who's out.

Everything is high pressure. Human nature can't endure much more!

Sounds like something from this morning's newspaper, right? Wrong. It appeared over 150 years ago—June 16, 1833, to be exact—in the *Atlantic Journal*. Back in those "good ol' days."

Do you have any idea what the headlines were in the *Boston Globe* in mid-November 1857? If you can't remember back that far, let me refresh your memory.

ENERGY CRISIS LOOMS

The subhead suggested that the world may go dark, owing to a frightening scarcity of whale blubber!

Who says "the good ol' days" were all that good?

Back in the forties I distinctly recall our soldiers, sailors, and marines dying by the thousands as a world war raged on either side of the globe. I remember enduring Houston heat without air-conditioning. Some of my childhood friends were crippled for life from polio.

Further back in the thirties—the decade in which I was born—the shadow of the Great Depression brought scarcity and despair to every state in the Union. Great times, huh?

My *dad's* "good ol' days" were even worse. That was when you had to start your car with a crank . . . when homes had no indoor plumbing . . . when everybody in the family took baths in No. 2 washtubs . . . when travel abroad took long and treacherous days by ship across oceans . . . when horses died by the dozens in New York because of a cholera plague . . . when rain turned streets into a bog. I could go on. Now I ask you, were those days really all that good?

You see, everything depends on one's perspective. Charles Dickens' now-famous line still applies: "It was the best of times. It was the worst of times."[20] Some look back and remember only the best of times—an easier pace, closer ties, and more honest relationships. Others see the inconveniences, the obsolescence, the prejudices, and inefficiency. When you stop long enough to think objectively, you realize that *no time* is ideal, necessitating the importance of flexing with the times.

How Times Change!

Speaking of "times," do you remember the statement recorded in the ancient writings of Daniel the prophet?

Let the name of God be blessed forever and ever,
For wisdom and power belong to Him.
And it is He who changes the times and the epochs;
He removes kings and establishes kings;
He gives wisdom to wise men,
And knowledge to men of understanding (Daniel 2:20–21).

What assurance! It is not mere chance or blind fate that determines the sweeping changes that impact every generation. Our sovereign God takes full responsibility. He tells us it is He who affects change. And the good news is this: When changes occur, they are never out of His control!

My times are in Thy hand . . . (Psalm 31:15).

If we truly believed that, changes would not be nearly so difficult to accept. Nor would they cause us such anxiety. Everything from modern inventions to global alterations could be taken in stride because He—our faithful God—is still in control. Nothing surprises or threatens Him. *Nothing!* He is in charge of all seasons and epochs. No president takes the oath of office without God's nodding and saying, "That is My will." No king reigns without God's saying, "That is the one I allow." No advancement in technology or science catches Him off guard. If you believe God is sovereign, then you cannot believe He is ever out of date. He lives and rules in timelessness.

Frankly, I find that exciting. The population explosion continues precisely as He has planned. Did you know that it was not until 1850 that our world reached the one billion mark? By 1930 we reached two billion. It took only thirty more years for the world's population to reach three billion. We have now arrived at five billion. Statisticians tell us that by the end of the twentieth century we'll have seven billion. But let me remind you, our population growth, no matter how rapid, is still in God's hands.

Are you ready for another mind-boggling change? Let's take the increased number of published books. If you go back to 1500, you return to the beginning of printed materials. Not much was done with published books by 1900 . . . by then there were only 35,000 available. Today? Over 400,000 books are published in the United States alone . . . *every year*. That averages over a thousand new books published per day just in America.

And consider the enlargement of knowledge. If we could measure knowledge by space, all of human knowledge from the beginning of time to 1845 could be measured in one inch. From 1845 to 1945 it would expand to three inches. From 1945 to today the growth spurt in knowledge is phenomenal. It could reach the height of the Washington Monument. Still, our times are in His hands. Contrary to popular opinion, God understands nuclear energy, the microchip, and rocket science.

I should also mention speed. Until 1800 the top speed was twenty miles an hour as people traveled on horseback. There were prophets of doom back then when someone mentioned traveling fast. I read somewhere that one of the earlier critics of speed was convinced if you traveled one hundred miles an hour, you'd stutter for the rest of your life. Your mind would leave you, your emotions would break down. The human body couldn't tolerate such speed. Nevertheless, with the arrival of the railroad train, almost overnight we jumped to one hundred miles an hour. Amazing! Nobody started stuttering.

By 1952 the passenger jet aircraft could travel three hundred miles an hour. By 1979 the more advanced aircraft reached six hundred miles an hour. But the manned space flight had long since set a much greater record. Back in 1961 the astronauts were traveling in orbit no less than sixteen thousand miles an hour.

It occurred to me not long ago that my father saw the full panorama of that transportation era during his lifetime. Between

1892 and 1980, he saw one of the first cars and lived to witness by television the launching of rockets and the landing on the moon. While thinking of speed, one forward-thinking author writes:

> In the year 2020, automobiles probably will be powered by an advanced battery pack for the short runs to and from offices and shopping. For the longer trips, cars will be powered by liquid-hydrogen engines. The exhaust from our future highway vehicles will be pure oxygen and steam, which are the by-products from burning liquid hydrogen. In effect, there will be tens of millions of rolling vacuum cleaners sucking the smog out of the cities and replacing it with air cleaner than the air above the Colorado Rockies. A big semi-trailer will roar down the freeway, belching clouds of pure oxygen out of its stacks. There will be a sticker on the back of the truck with a new slogan: "Teamsters for Clean Air!"

The same author then describes a senior prom of the future:

> In the twenty-first century it will be common for proms to be held in foreign countries like Australia, which will be a popular choice. Australia will be a half-orbital shuttle run in twenty-nine minutes with a shuttle-busload of formally attired space travelers enjoying the spectacular, but brief panoramic view. They will go to Australia for the prom, but probably sneak over to Hong Kong for the after-prom, telling us they were in Australia with the chaperones the whole evening. Some things never change through the generations![21]

I could include numerous other changes. If you are in the medical or dental profession, you know many of them. To name a few: the ability to select the sex of the newborn; creation of life in the test tube; growth of fetuses in artificial wombs; the development of ova and sperm banks; elimination of tooth decay by welding enamel on teeth with the laser beam; spot welding of the retina of the eye; the extended use of the bloodless knife in surgery; the increased use of artificial organs, such as plastic corneas for the eye, metallic bones, Dacron arteries, artificial hearts, and computerized electronic muscles; the development of synthetic food, even ocean farming (not to mention the probability of undersea cities); general immunization of the world against common diseases; experiments in human hibernation; the development of effective appetite and weight-control programs.

May I ask rather bluntly: In light of these remarkable changes (all of which are in God's hands), why does the church remain riveted to yesterday? I repeat my theme: The church has stumbled along long enough. We have been reticent to change long enough. Instead of hesitating any longer, we need to get in step. As those who stand by the Creator and Source of all knowledge and invention, we need to see changes as friends rather than resist them as enemies.

One of my mentors loves to talk about his church back in the Midwest where he grew up. Somebody introduced the flannelgraph in an adult Sunday school class, one of the trendy visual aids commonly used in the business world during that era. The poor guy was verbally crucified! He was called before the board and severely lectured. "How *dare* you contaminate our church with this worldly method!"

Can you believe it? All he did was introduce a flannelgraph and use it as a teaching aid. You'd think he had released a trunk full of cobras!

Let me share a couple of thoughts regarding our times. *The possibilities these changes bring are thrilling.* Think of the excitement it brings to put an unwritten language quickly into the hands of the people. I can remember the days when we deposited a couple in the jungle and hoped that within a decade or more they could provide one book of the New Testament for that tribe . . . handwritten on a tablet. With the help of computers, that task can now be accomplished in a matter of months—followed by an entire Bible in just a few years.

Think of the possibilities in rapid travel. Years ago you couldn't get from America to Europe in less than twelve to fourteen long days across the Atlantic. Now we can do it in hours. Someday, in *minutes*. Think of what that will do to world evangelization. Thanks to the electronic media, an evangelist can now stand before a camera and, with the help of a satellite in space, be seen *all around the world* in split seconds. Live. Back in the so-called "good ol' days" that was strictly Flash Gordon and Buck Rogers stuff.

Here is a second thought. *Such changes, if we are not careful, will be threatening to many.* If you are a hold-the-line, rigid-thinking traditionalist, change will seem threatening, and you will be tempted to resist it. For some reason this is especially true among evangelicals. We can be the worst when it comes to opening our eyes and seeing the opportunities staring back at us. Even with Jesus Christ, the greatest religion innovator the world has ever known, standing right beside us.

As a church in the twentieth century, only a few years shy of the twenty-first, let's not be threatened by the changes of our times. We must continually monitor and evaluate our methods. It helps me to remember that none of the methods we employ is sacred. Unless a particular method is set forth in Scripture as *the* unchanging method God says we are to use, it is temporary. That means it can be altered or discarded, replaced by a better and more efficient method.

I'll be honest with you. One of my great concerns for the up-and-coming young minister is that he or she might be a traditionalist with regard to methods. I fear that many of those who graduate with a solid, biblically based theology will be straight-jacketed with the times in which they are trained.

Seminaries *must* remain on the cutting edge. I have a personal concern about those who teach communication in seminaries today. How easy to think as a traditionalist and teach dated styles! The communication style of the fifties is altogether different than communicating in the nineties. You do not reach and win an audience today by using a dogmatic Walter Winchell approach, popular forty or fifty years ago. Today's audience requires a different style. Effective communicators and interested listeners are learners together. The young student today has witnessed the best in communication long before he reached graduate school. Among other things, he has watched those methods on television and in films. In this hotly competitive, market-driven world of ours, countless voices seek to win a hearing. Methods must continually be evaluated and, when necessary, changed. Yes, even in churches.

I love the way Edith Wharton expresses the secret of staying alive in her autobiography, *A Backward Glance*:

> In spite of illness, in spite even of the archenemy sorrow: one *can* remain alive long past the usual date of disintegration if one is unafraid of change, insatiable in intellectual curiosity, interested in big things, and happy in small ways.

Don't miss the first of those four: unafraid of change.

But Some Things Will Never Change

Right about now I can feel the vibes. A few of you are beginning to wonder if I am implying that we change everything. No! There are some things, quite candidly, we are to keep our hands off, regardless of how modern the era.

To illustrate this, consider something the psalmist wrote in Psalm 11. David, no doubt, is feeling threatened. Saul is after him. David has found a hiding place in some cleft of the rock, perhaps a cave, where he wrote the psalm. Maybe it was raining that day. Perhaps it was one of those gray-slush days when everything seemed bleak and purposeless. We can feel the emotions in the first two verses:

> In the LORD I take refuge;
> How can you say to my soul,
> "Flee as a bird to your mountain;

For, behold, the wicked bend the bow,
They make ready their arrow upon the string,
To shoot in darkness at the upright in heart" (11:1–2).

He says to his Lord, "In You I take *refuge*." The Hebrew word suggests a place to hide. David found comfort hiding in his relationship with his God.

No doubt he senses the Lord saying to him: "Trust Me. I'm protecting you." And so, in fear, he answers back,

> *How can you say to my soul,*
> *"Flee as a bird to your mountain."*

"I mean, Saul is after me, Lord. I can hear my name used in cursing outside my cave. I can't run to some mountain."

> *"For, behold, the wicked bend the bow,*
> *They make ready their arrow upon the string,*
> *To shoot in darkness at the upright in heart."*

In those days, night-fighting was among the most treacherous of attacks. David knows he is not safe, even after darkness falls. Finally, in quasi-panic, he asks the Lord,

> *"If the foundations are destroyed,*
> *What can the righteous do?"* (v. 3).

Now that is a realistic and relevant point. "Lord, in You I find refuge. But, surrounded by the wicked with no relief in sight, I fear the shaking of the foundations."

Those of us who live in California can identify with that. I have witnessed numerous hurricanes in South Texas. I have driven through blizzards in New England and endured four-day storms in the middle of the ocean. I have been through a firebomb threat on a commercial airliner, and other equally threatening circumstances. I have also had my life and my family members' lives threatened by crazed individuals. None of those fears, however, come near the fear of the earth's foundations shaking beneath me. When it comes to fears, earthquakes are number one!

But David is not writing about a physical earthquake here. No, he is saying, "Lord, what can the righteous do if everything is up for grabs? What do we do if *everything* changes so much that even You begin to change? What can the righteous do then?" Ever thought that? I certainly have.

It is wonderful to find later in the Scriptures an answer to a question asked earlier in Scripture. Here is a case in point. The answer to David's question is found in the last letter Paul wrote— 2 Timothy.

One of Paul's long-term friends was a younger man named Timothy. He was probably in his forties by the time this letter was penned to him. The two men had traveled together, grown together, learned together, suffered together. Now that Paul is in a dungeon about to say goodbye to life and Timothy is taking up the torch to carry on as a pastor in Ephesus, the elder writes the younger a letter, actually *two* of them. This is Paul's swan song, his last will and testament. If a person's last words are his most significant, here we have Paul's. He told Timothy that in light of the changing times:

> *Remind them of these things, and solemnly charge them in the presence of God not to wrangle about words, which is useless, and leads to the ruin of the hearers* (2 Timothy 2:14).

Timothy is to remind his congregation of the timeless truths of God. Some of those truths have been mentioned by Paul in the previous paragraphs of his letter. Here, he is urging his friend to major on the majors, not the minors . . . not to get caught up in word battles and verbal arguments, but to stay at the essential issues that are worth his time and effort. He then urges Timothy to—

> *Be diligent to present yourself approved to God as a workman who does not need to be ashamed, handling accurately the word of truth* (v. 15).

Truth. The word of truth . . . clearly a reference to God's holy Word, the Bible. He says, in effect, "Timothy, you've not merely been given a Book of sermons, but more importantly a Book of truth. God's truths are broad and magnificent. They will literally change lives. Therefore, my friend, stay in the Book. Give your flock the timeless truths of Scripture."

> *But avoid worldly and empty chatter, for it will lead to further ungodliness, and their talk will spread like gangrene.*

(Today we would say, "Their talk will spread like cancer.")

> *Among them are Hymenaeus and Philetus, men who have gone astray from the truth saying that the resurrection has already taken place, and thus they upset the faith of some* (vv. 16–18).

These men had strayed from the truth of Scripture and, as a result, influenced others who followed their ungodly example. Now the climax:

> *Nevertheless, the firm foundation of God stands, having this seal, "The Lord knows those who are His," and, "Let everyone who names the name of the Lord abstain from wickedness"* (v. 19).

I love that! God's foundation stands firm. It is unshakable and unchangeable. Ken Taylor paraphrases this same verse in *The Living Bible: But God's truth stands firm like a great rock, and nothing can shake it.*

Count on this: There will be more earthquakes, but there will never be a truthquake. There will never be a day when God will come back on the scene and say, "You know, I've been rethinking My Book. Some of those truths I wrote about Jesus, well, I need to rewrite all that. Also, a few of the character traits about Me and some of those doctrines in My Book need to be updated." He will never do that. His truth is more solid than a thousand-ton mound of granite.

As a matter of fact, God has said in this verse that there are two seals; one invisible and one visible. Together, they prove His truth will never be shaken.

We know the foundation of God stands firm and unchanging because of the invisible seal of His promise. What has been writ-

ten in the Book will remain unchanged in that Book. Securely
sealed and absolutely safe.

The other guarantee is visible. Just look around and observe
"those who are His." The lifestyles of the righteous are proof God's
foundation stands unchanged. They may be only a remnant, but
the righteous are there in every generation.

What am I getting at? It's simple. Our challenge is to stay up
with the times, to serve our generation, yet in no way alter the
truths of His Word. Styles and methods change and must be kept
up to date. But truth? It is timeless. Not subject to change. The
whole point of this chapter could be stated in one sentence. *We
are to be willing to leave the familiar without disturbing the essentials.*
To minister effectively the church must wake up to what changes
. . . and what doesn't.

Charles Wesley understood this even in 1762, when he wrote:

> *A charge to keep I have,*
> *A God to glorify,*
> *A never-dying soul to save,*
> *And fit it for the sky.*
> *To serve the present age,*
> *My calling to fulfill;*
> *O may it all my powers engage,*
> *To do my Master's will!*[22]

Don't miss that relevant statement: "To serve the present age."
As far back as the mid-eighteenth century, Wesley saw the value
of staying current. Serving the present age need not preclude our
serving God.

Many evangelical churches of this generation are making a
grave error. Afraid of change, they have somehow connected yes-
teryear's methodology with the timeless truth of the Scriptures.
There is the strange idea that if we hold true to Scripture, we must
resist any alteration of method—as if integrity of biblical stance
requires rigidity of practical style. Not so. If there are modern
inventions that will help us get the message out more powerfully,

more quickly, and more effectively, why hesitate using them? If they work, if they don't compromise our theology and contaminate our message, why not employ them?

At the same time, there are dangers in embracing something simply because it is new. We get burned thinking that which is modern and futuristic is safe because it is in the hands of modern, futuristic, safe people. Not necessarily.

Two thoughts come to mind. First, we need to continue hearing what God says as we adjust our lives to the times in which we live. Second, we need to keep believing what God says more than any other voice in the future. By doing both we stay flexible and effective in our approach while remaining godly and pure in lifestyle.

Let me show you why this distinction is vital. Consider the kind of people on the horizon of today and tomorrow. Second Timothy 3 pulls no punches:

> *But realize this, that in the last days difficult times will come. For men will be lovers of self, lovers of money, boastful, arrogant, revilers, disobedient to parents, ungrateful, unholy, unloving, irreconcilable, malicious gossips, without selfcontrol, brutal, haters of good, treacherous, reckless, conceited, lovers of pleasure rather than lovers of God; holding to a form of godliness, although they have denied its power; and avoid such men as these* (vv. 1–5).

How easy to think that if it is futuristic and innovative, fast-moving and modern, it is going to be better. Not so. The future will include savage times. (I will develop that fact in much greater detail in chapter 7.) We will build enough weapons to kill ourselves more quickly. We will invent vehicles with sufficient speed to run over whomever we please, because ungodly people of the future will be haters of that which is good. That is why God's unchanging message of love and forgiveness is important and must not be altered. Modern futuristic humanity will still suffer the effects of the same disease—total depravity.

Who can handle the future? Only those who have their hearts right. The rest will turn it against themselves and us. That explains why I don't think anybody is better equipped to handle the responsibilities of the future than the informed, alert Christian. We have all the built-in self-controls needed. I have often said that God is not in the heavens hanging on for dear life, thinking, "What am I going to do with this world that's speeding by?" Trust me, none of our futuristic stuff, no matter how sophisticated, bothers Him. He understands and remains in full control. When He is good and ready, it will be curtains . . . lights out. Until He changes things on Planet Earth, present and future times will remain personally difficult and morally degenerate.

Nice-sounding, even inviting heresies will be more and more in vogue. There will be increasingly more who will follow the film star who solved her struggles by buying into the New Age movement. There will be a groundswell of searchers following her and other gurus. The blind will continue to lead the blind. Not only did Jesus speak of this (please read Matthew 15:1–14), but Paul addressed it more than a few times. For example:

Evil men and impostors will proceed from bad to worse, deceiving and being deceived (2 Timothy 3:13).

Count on it: The future, with all its exciting discoveries and inventions, will include an increasing number of deceivers.

THE MAJOR INGREDIENT FOR SURVIVAL

Do you want to know what it will take to keep the proper balance between staying up with our times and standing firm on God's truth? Discernment. Without discernment it will be easy to get sucked into the system. Discernment will act as a watchdog to keep us from getting lost in the morass of tomorrow's depravity and deception even as we keep pace with its advancements. Webster defines *discernment* as "the power to see what is not evident to the average mind . . . accuracy, especially in reading character or motive." Discernment, in my opinion, will be all-the-more valuable as we stay in touch with our times.

What works for us as individual Christians will work for the church. The church that sits around frowning at the future, doing little more than polishing yesterday's apples, will become a church lacking in relevance and excitement. At the same time, the church that softens its stand theologically and alters Scripture to fit the future's style, will lose its power. Remember this: We must be willing to leave the familiar without disturbing the essentials. The secret, I repeat, is discernment.

TWO SUGGESTIONS FOR KEEPING OUR BALANCE

What we may need is a couple of suggestions on how to stay on the tightrope of truth without being blown off by the strong winds of heresy which are sure to come.

First, *changing times require the willingness to retool and flex where needed.* You may have a certain style of worship that has worked well in the past. You may have used it for years. Trust me, you need to keep rethinking that whole ball of wax. Is it still the best approach to use in light of the times in which we are living? Will it compromise Scripture to alter your style? Probably not. How willing are you to flex? How open to change?

I remember an incident that occurred in the church I pastored for almost twenty-three years. Several of the old guard warned me, "You allow multiple services and you're going to ruin the unity of the church." They spoke with sincere concern. They had enjoyed a closeness of fellowship since the church began. For over fifteen years the church always had one worship service in the morning and one worship service in the evening. Those who had been entrenched in that style felt threatened with the risk of change: "You just can't have more than one, or we'll lose what we've got."

What they meant was that we would lose the "neighborhood closeness we've always had." They were hesitant to face the fact that we were changing into a metropolitan ministry. Growth required innovative thinking. We had to do something. The crowded conditions could not be ignored. By the way, we have started over half a dozen other churches in our history, so no one could say we hadn't tried to flex. But we were still turning people away. Adding multiple services became our best option. Churches have to retool and flex. I am pleased to say that the congregation "tolerated" the additional worship services . . . and later agreed it was our best solution. Today we cannot imagine what it would be like to have a single morning worship gathering.

Second, *changeless truths require the discipline to resist and fight when necessary.* No amount of futuristic technology or modernistic advancement gives us the right to deny God's Book or alter its truths. The Scriptures give us our standard. That's a given. The truths of God are our sure foundation.

There was no more security or hope in the "good ol' days" than there will be in the "bad new days." But by the grace and mercy of God, as we stay open to the need to change and flex, we'll survive.

Check that. We won't simply survive. We will triumph!

1.   Scary newspaper headlines and grim evening news broadcasts cause us to shake our heads in disbelief at times. Some of us allow those sad and shocking stories from around the globe to put a knot in our stomachs, robbing us of the peace and joy that belong to us in Christ. If I'm writing to a "news junkie" who can't leave those headlines alone, let me make an observation and a suggestion. First of all, God never intended us to carry the weight of this broken world on our own shoulders. Only His shoulders are large enough for that task—and He *is* in control! Give the weight and anxiety back to Him. Let me suggest that you give "equal time" to the grand and glorious psalms that remind us of God's power, eternity, and love. If you watch half an hour of news, spend the same amount of time in the Psalms. Give God the last word!

2.   If you've been involved in a particular ministry for a long while, you may find yourself stuck in comfortable but time-worn methodology. Are you open to learning new ways and fresh expressions—without compromising timeless truth? Check into a few resources to see what innovations may have developed in your ministry niche. You might begin by talking with individuals who minister in your area of interest at a large metropolitan church. You might also find help in some new books or periodicals at your local Christian or Bible college bookstore.

3.   Draw a line down the center of a sheet of paper, from top to bottom. Now think through all of the ministry activities of your church in a given week. On the left side of the paper, list those activities that are biblical and remain permanent priorities. On the right side, try to list a few of the traditional methods your

church employs that might be reviewed and/or updated in the coming months and years. Discuss your list with your spouse or a Christian friend, strategizing how you might become a *positive* force for change in one or more of those areas.

MINISTERING IN THE LAST DAYS

ow about a quick quiz?

We've been going at these matters rather intensely, so maybe it's time to review where we've been and have a little fun at the same time. It's our goal to remember who the church is in the sight of God and of Jesus Christ. And a little test can help determine if you've really been reading or if you're asleep under the book you've got in your hands. I promise I'll stay with the big-picture questions. To make it easier, I will limit the quiz to multiple-choice questions. Circle your answer to each of the following questions:

1. We learned in chapter 1 that the primary purpose of the church is:

    a.   To be a lighthouse of hope in the community

    b.   To glorify God

    c.   To help the hungry and the hurting

    d.   To give teenagers a place to go on Saturday night.

2. In the second chapter I suggested the acronym "WIFE" to help us remember the basic objectives of the church. "W" represents worship. "F" represents fellowship. "E" represents expression. What does "I" represent?

    a.   Image
    b.   Involvement
    c.   Instruction
    d.   Indebtedness

  3. I then began to address a church's style. As I wrote about the importance of a "contagious" style, I suggested four characteristics: A church needs to be B____ IN CONTENT, AUTHENTIC IN NATURE, GRACIOUS IN ATTITUDE, AND RELEVANT IN APPROACH. What word belongs in the blank?
    a.   Bold
    b.   Basic
    c.   Biblical
    d.   Boring

  4. In chapter 5 I wrote about the differences between a "neighborhood" church and a "metropolitan" church. To illustrate the value of delegation, we turned to the Old Testament and found a classic example of one person who confronted another about his need to delegate the time-consuming responsibilities of his office. Who were these two individuals?
    a.   Samson and Delilah
    b.   Jonathan and David
    c.   Sarah and Abraham
    d.   Jethro and Moses

  5. We just finished the chapter having to do with change. We considered the value of staying flexible and open in some areas, yet remaining firm and sure in others. I offered one central statement, which you may remember. We must be willing to leave the familiar without disturbing the essentials. We looked into both the Old and New Testaments and found the answer to a question. The psalmist wrote "If the _____ are destroyed, what can the righteous do?" Paul stated the _____ stands firm. What is it that will stand firm forever?
    a.   The *doxology* at the beginning of a worship service
    b.   The *methods* of evangelism we adopt as a church
    c.   The *foundation* of God

...en they will deliver you to tribulation, and will kill you, and ...u will be hated by all nations on account of My name. And ...that time many will fall away and will deliver up one anoth- ...and hate one another. And many false prophets will arise, ...d will mislead many. And because lawlessness is increased, ...st people's love will grow cold" (vv. 3–12).

...t me ask again, Will our times get better or will they get ...? The answer is painfully obvious. On this old planet there ... a dramatic crescendo of wickedness. If I were asked to give ...ightforward analysis of what we should expect, based on ...teaching, I would say: First, conditions will worsen; second, ...s will weaken; third, morals will wane.

...tions Will Worsen

...ternational conflicts will not only grow and abound, they ...crease in such measure that some nations will no longer tol- ...other nations. As we're going to read a little later in the ...er, people will not only have conflicts, they will become ...ncilable. They will refuse to negotiate in a civil manner. ... talking nose-to-nose hostility.

...hen Dean Rusk was secretary of state under President John ...dy during the Cuban missile crisis, he commented, "We're ...l-to-eyeball, and I think the other fellow just blinked." As ...asses, there will be more staring and less understanding . . . ...tubborn entrenching and less frequent reasoning.

...nile down inside every time I see the imprint on the postage ..."Pray for peace." There will *never* be international peace ...Christ reigns supreme. With all good intentions, our states- ...nd women strive for peace, but, alas, it is a futile pursuit. ...nger we live on this old earth, the more it will resemble the ...s tossing of the sea.

...chnical knowledge may abound and reach new heights. We ...velop ways to help people live longer, but the deeper ques- ... will they *want* to? More than ever are voting "No, I want

d. The *announcements* in the middle
    gatherings

Okay, it's time to grade your quiz. Lookin
tions, the correct answers are 1-B, 2-C, 3-C, 4
do? If you got all five, I commend you. You'
of who the church is and why God's plan for
changed in twenty centuries. If you missed t
you need glasses!

GENERAL EVALUATION: WHAT WE S

No matter what you made on that quiz,
question nobody would miss. True or false: 7
than they have ever been. Without a doub
you would agree, spiritually, morally, ethica
times have never been worse. Only the blir
otherwise. I don't believe I have spoken wi
past twenty-five years who really believes t
ter and better. The fact is, they're getting ir

Jesus Himself taught that this would occ
loguing with the disciples, He answered
quently giving them answers they didn't
records one of the final discourses of our Sav
to His death and resurrection. In this partic
disciples are concerned about the end times

> *And as He was sitting on the Mount of*
> *came to Him privately, saying, "Tell us, u*
> *be, and what will be the sign of Your comi*
> *the age?" And Jesus answered and said to*
> *no one misleads you. For many will come*
> *'I am the Christ,' and will mislead many. .*
> *ing of wars and rumors of wars; see that yc*
> *for those things must take place, but that i*
> *nation will rise against nation, and kingd*
> *and in various places there will be famir*
> *But all these things are merely the begir*

out." Check the increasing suicide rate—even among teenagers. It is frightening.

Homes Will Weaken

Families will continue to disintegrate. No need to restate the obvious. There isn't a person reading these lines who could say, "I know of no one divorced." Every one of us knows someone who has gone through that chamber of horrors. Some of you have endured it against your own desire. I can hear you sigh, "I never wanted it, but I am a victim of it. My family weakened, the relationship fractured, and the very thing I swore would never happen in my home has occurred. And it has taken its toll on my children." Delinquency is now so bad, teachers with tenure are leaving their profession. It is no exaggeration to state that the fractured family is now a national epidemic.

Morals Will Wane

What once made us blush, we now watch with ease on the television set. Back in 1939 a simple four-letter word uttered in a film made front-page headlines. That word and far worse are now commonly heard in the media.

It would be easy for those of us who still blush to think things are way out of hand and have gotten out of control. We may be thinking, "God must be wringing His hands, wondering, 'What will I do with this world?'" But as we saw in the previous chapter, such is not the case. As a matter of fact, "the firm foundation of God stands" (2 Timothy 2:19). While none of this is out of His control, it grieves our Lord to say that most people's love will grow cold.

Nevertheless [I love the way the verse begins] . . .
Nevertheless, the firm foundation of God stands.

Truth will win. Even though it seems, as James Russell Lowell wrote, we see "Truth forever on the scaffold, Wrong forever on the throne."[23] God's way will win!

Nevertheless, the firm foundation of God stands, having this seal, "The Lord knows those who are His," and, "Let everyone who names the name of the Lord abstain from wickedness."

The question isn't, Will things get difficult? (They will.) Nor, Is God in control? (He is.) The greater question is, How do we live and minister in a world that has lost its way? What does a church do to make a dent? What will it take to make us remember who we are and who stands beside us so that we can impact a world speeding faster than ever in the wrong direction?

What's the answer? Is it to build our walls thicker and higher? Should we lock our church door and distribute the keys exclusively to our own to guarantee protection of our own little pocket of purity? Obviously, no. What then do we do? How do we make a difference in these last days?

In the same Scripture we examined in chapter 6, we will find an answer to that question. In fact, we'll find some answers that are not only correct, they are relevant and insightful. In 2 Timothy 3 we read one of the most vivid accounts of end-time wickedness found in all the Bible. In my opinion it is second only to Romans 1 when it comes to an unvarnished description of depravity. The helpful dimension of 2 Timothy 3 is the practical instruction it includes on how to respond when facing such times.

SCRIPTURAL INSTRUCTION: HOW WE MUST RESPOND

Let's not hurry through these words of instruction. Paul begins quite realistically as he informs his long-time friend, Timothy:

But realize this, that in the last days difficult times will come (2 Timothy 3:1).

One wonders why the aging apostle would begin by stating what seems redundant. Of course Timothy realized the days were difficult! Martyrs were dropping like flies. At that time it was more than unpopular to be known as a Christian—it was potentially fatal. Back then, when you made your faith known, the government took notice. So did the neighbors. You paid a terrible price for your faith. Why then does Paul say, "Realize this"?

Here's why: He knew Timothy. Timothy had the type of temperament that needed to be stirred up. On more than one occasion Paul admonished his friend to "stir up the gift" which God had given him. I take it that he was a bit more passive than his mentor, which caused the wise old teacher to say to the younger, "Get with it! Stay alert!"

Timothy might have been the type to think that although times were bad right then, they would probably ease off—"It isn't going to be permanently difficult. The storm will blow over if I lie low." To set the record straight, Paul warns, "Realize this, Timothy, it is not going to lighten up. This last-days lifestyle is here to stay."

BRIEF EXPOSÉ OF LAST-DAYS' DEPRAVITY

Look again at the words "*difficult* times will come." The term is translated from a Greek word seldom used in Scripture. It means more than hard; perhaps "harsh" is better, or "hard to deal with." The King James Version of the Bible translates it *grievous*, an excellent rendering. I found it helpful to note that the same Greek term is used in Matthew 8:28 to describe the appearance and actions of two men who were demonized. In that verse the term is translated "exceedingly violent." As I mentioned earlier, it is not too extreme to render the word "savage." Let's do that:

But realize this, that in the last days savage times will come.

Why linger so long on one word? Because of one other word: Reality. No amount of reflection on the glories of the marriage supper of the Lamb can undo the fact that we live in an age of violence that will continue, right up until Christ takes His Bride home. And to make matters worse, we live in a day when we are surrounded by a whistle-in-the-dark, positive-thinking mentality. While I firmly believe in the importance of thinking positively, I think it can be taken to an extreme when we fail to think *realistically.*

If we truly believe these are "savage times . . . exceedingly violent," then we will not be shocked by any event or newspaper headline. It may grieve us or embarrass us, but it should never surprise us, since God has warned us that in the last days there will be times that are hard to deal with, harsh, and marked by violence.

One half-page article that I read in a newspaper could easily have boggled my mind. It was the account of a man who murdered each member of his family. He left some of them dead in the home or in the trunk of a car for more than a day. The murders went beyond his family. The list went on to include several close friends and employees. How many in all? Fourteen. Savage times are upon us.

Another article I saw told of a man who sprayed bullets across a schoolyard with a military assault rifle, killing and wounding a number of small children. We can hardly imagine anything more violent than murdering innocent children. As I wrote this book there were several scandalous trials going on in the county where I live. Each involved a defendant being tried for multiple murders. The lengthy trials contained vivid and shameful accounts of rape, stabbings, dismembering, sodomy, homosexuality, drug abuse, child molestation, and a half dozen other sociopathic crimes that included acts so immoral they almost curdle your blood. And each man on trial sat there absolutely placid, sometimes with an eerie grin on his face. There was no sense of remorse or apparent shame. In exceedingly violent times there will be a greater absence of guilt, stronger rationalization, and less emphasis on the punishment of evildoers.

Even our freeways have become fast lanes of terror as gun-toting drivers don't hesitate to shoot another driver simply because he cut in on his lane of traffic. Neither time nor space allows me to include the sordid details of other crimes so hideous we must force ourselves to believe they were committed by fellow human beings. Face it, we live in a crazed era.

Realize this, Christian. Be aware of this, church.

In such savage times relatively few will consistently walk with God. Fewer marital partners will remain faithful to their vows and stay committed to marriage. It will be harder and harder to rear a family that takes God seriously. Realize that! Such a realization will call for a greater sense of intensity and deeper determination among the people of God. Because there will be mass killings, gang wars, an increase in sexual perversions, a growing number of unethical practices, and domestic violence the likes of which the world has not seen, our walk with God must intensify.

Paul gets painfully specific.

> *For men will be lovers of self, lovers of money, boastful, arrogant, revilers, disobedient to parents, ungrateful, unholy, unloving, irreconcilable . . . (vv. 2–3).*

You may question why your offended neighbor would not come to terms with you over that mild offense. You wonder why he or she sued you rather than simply walking over, knocking on your front door, and requesting that the two of you talk things over? You wonder why the fellow who slipped and fell in your store was not willing to talk to you instead of his attorney? Or when you bumped the guy's car in front of you, you wonder why he wasn't willing to shrug it off as a minor accident and negotiate the difference? The next thing you knew, you were served papers. Why? "Men will be . . . irreconcilable"! *Realize this.*

Let's hold our breath and read on:

> *. . . malicious gossips, without self-control, brutal, haters of good, treacherous, reckless, conceited, lovers of pleasure rather than lovers of God; holding to a form of godliness, although they have denied its power; and avoid such men as these. For among them are those who enter into households and captivate weak women weighed down with sins, led on by various impulses, always learning and never able to come to the knowledge of the truth. And just as Jannes and Jambres opposed Moses. . . .*

(Those two men were magicians in Pharaoh's court who attempted to ape the living God and fake His power in the presence of

Pharaoh. As Moses did his miracles by God's power, Jannes and Jambres did theirs by the adversary's power.)

> *And just as Jannes and Jambres opposed Moses, so these men also oppose the truth* . . . (vv. 3–8).

In the last days they won't passively ignore truth, they will aggressively oppose it. *Realize that.*

Paul is shaking us by the shoulders, saying "Christian! Christian! Even though you truly love God—as do others who stand with you—stop living in a fantasy world, thinking that everything will be nice and neat if you just relocate in a more peaceful spot, or in a spot where people even talk religion. Ungodliness will still be there. There is no Fantasy Island." Wherever you settle, there will be

> . . . *men of depraved mind, rejected as regards the faith* (v. 8).

Look closely. So far as the mind is concerned, there will be depravity, corruption. As to their faith, rejection. They will be counterfeit. Tried and found wanting.

Right about now the situation is beginning to seem hopeless. I feel the need for a little relief, don't you? We find it in verse 9. Paul, knowing that Timothy would take his words seriously, gave him a little breathing room by addressing the young man personally.

> *But* [Timothy, don't worry] *they will not make further progress; for their folly will be obvious to all, as also that of those two* [Jannes and Jambres] *came to be* (v. 9).

He is saying something like, "Timothy, realize this, there will still be some who will see through it all. There will still be those in the family of God who will discern truth from error. Not everyone will get sucked into the system."

John R. W. Stott mentions an easily forgotten fact:

> We sometimes get distressed in our day—rightly and understandably—by the false teachers who oppose the truth and trouble the church, especially by the sly and slip-

pery methods of backdoor religious traders. But we need have no fear, even if a few weak people may be taken in, even if falsehood becomes fashionable. For there is something patently spurious about heresy, and something self-evidently true about the truth. Error may spread and be popular for a time. But it will not get very far. In the end it is bound to be exposed, and the truth is sure to be vindicated. This is a clear lesson of church history. Numerous heresies have arisen, and some have seemed likely to triumph. But today they are largely of antiquarian interest. God has preserved his truth in the church.[24]

Isn't it a wonderful comfort to remind ourselves that God's books of divine justice are not closed every night? It gives me a growing sense of inner peace to remember that God's chapters are still being written. He has not yet said, "The end." Admittedly, the ever increasing groundswell of heresy, mixed with moral impurity and physical violence, almost causes me to shudder. I occasionally wonder if it is going to overwhelm us. Then when I find these quiet reminders in God's Book, it is remarkable how reassured I feel. I am reminded anew that truth will prevail and ultimately triumph.

WISE ANSWERS TO ALL WHO MINISTER

With that gentle ray of hope, the apostle turns his attention directly to the man receiving the letter—and indirectly to all of us living in the last days. To him and to us he writes: "Here are some wise answers on how to survive the era in which you live. In a broader sense, here's how to abound."

He presents four specific answers. I will mention the first two as I conclude this chapter and save the last two for my next chapter.

First, *follow the model of the faithful.*

But you followed my teaching, conduct, purpose, faith, patience, love, perseverance, persecutions, and sufferings, such as happened to me at Antioch, at Iconium and at Lystra; what persecutions I endured, and out of them all the Lord delivered

*me! And indeed, all who desire to live godly in Christ Jesus will
be persecuted* (vv. 10–12).

Times are difficult, times are harsh, times are hard to deal with.
All this is true. "But you, Timothy . . ." This word "but" is a small
but powerful connective. It introduces a marked contrast. "There
are many (in fact, Jesus said 'most') who will grow cold. *But you,*
Timothy, you be different. You are not to be like 'the most.' You
dare not even be like 'the many.' You follow my model."

Do you have some models to follow? I am not referring to
saints in sculptured stone we place on pedestals and consider perfect. No. The models that sway our lives are very human—and
therefore imperfect. Nevertheless, they are great examples to us.
They motivate us to live better lives. They may have already lived
and died.

Your model may be an author whose book turned your life
around. As a result you have entered into a greater depth of life.
In a real sense, that author (whom you may never meet) is your
model.

Others of you may follow models who live near you. You've
studied that life up close and want to emulate similar virtues. The
more you study your model, the more you discover he or she is no
stranger to pain. Therefore, when you encounter similar pain, you
remember the persecutions your model has endured, which
encourages you to endure. That's what Paul is saying here. In fact,
pain and godliness are often connected.

Did you miss Paul's sober prediction?

*And indeed, all who desire to live godly in Christ Jesus will be
persecuted* (v. 12).

Speaking of models, isn't it interesting that in our decadent
era every attempt is being made to tear down those we once
admired? The political figures you have admired in our nation's
history are being systematically ripped apart so that none of them
will seem all that admirable—if certain critics have their way
about it. Let me encourage you not to allow that to happen. That
kind of cynical thinking leads to a lonely dead end.

I spoke with a man who hopes to move into the Senate or Congress. Ultimately, if God opens the door, he would seriously like to pursue becoming president of the United States. Right now he is virtually unknown. But locked in his mind are models, individuals who stand against wrong like a steer in a blizzard, people of the truth . . . people he can look up to and say, "That is what I want to be like." It fuels his fire. As he told me, "I am watching my models and taking my cues." I am encouraging him to continue reading biographies of great men and women.

The apostle says to Timothy, "You follow my example; if you do, you can make it."

If a personal testimony would help, consider my story. While in the Marine Corps en route to the Orient I came across a wonderful book, *Through Gates of Splendor*, about five missionaries who were martyred. I never knew those young men or their families. But from the testimony of five unknown men who literally gave their lives to reach the Aucas in Ecuador, this young Marine's life was turned around. They became models for me during a lonely, difficult era of my life. In many ways, their faithfulness kept me going. They became my silent voices of encouragement. They stand out in my mind as people worth following, worth reading, worth studying. I'm now much older than they were when they died. Though dead, they have spoken to me for over three decades. I still think of them and follow their example, though they left this world back in 1956.

When doing a little linguistic work on this word *follow*, it intrigued me to discover it is the same term Dr. Luke uses when he investigated all the facts before he wrote the Gospel that bears his name. After he checked out all the facts, he was able to write the story of the life of Christ. That particular term Luke used for investigating or carefully checking something out is the word translated in 2 Timothy 3:10 as "follow." So it doesn't mean we simply look from a distance and superficially admire someone's track record. It means we get as close as possible and make a careful investigation so as to discover the things that made that life great.

I'm spending extra time on this because I think it is part of last-days' survival training. If you just read and watch the media, you will turn down all models. You will be suspicious of every leader. Let's not let that happen to us! Just because a few have failed doesn't mean the ranks are full of nothing but charlatans, deceivers, and failures. Some are still people of truth . . . models of the faith worth following. Follow them!

Second, *return to the truth of the past.*

But evil men and impostors will proceed from bad to worse, deceiving and being deceived (v. 13).

There may be many impostors, but let's determine not to be one of them. Let's be different . . . as Timothy was. What was it that made Timothy different?

You, however, continue in the things you have learned and become convinced of, knowing from whom you have learned them; and that from childhood you have known the sacred writings which are able to give you the wisdom that leads to salvation through faith which is in Christ Jesus (vv. 14–15).

Hooray for Timothy's roots! If you go back to verse 5 of the first chapter in this letter, you will see that the sincere faith that ultimately marked Timothy's life first resided in his grandmother Lois and his mother Eunice. (Nothing is said of his father, who was probably a Greek and perhaps not a Christian.) It was Timothy's mother and maternal grandmother who shaped his early spiritual growth. His faith became sincere as he learned of Christ at their knees, sitting under their tutelage. Realizing the value of his grandmother's and mother's training, Paul exhorts Timothy to hang tough.

When thinking back over her life, my wife could easily identify with Timothy. Cynthia would say, "It was my mother and my mother's mother who shaped me." I would say, "It was my maternal grandfather." L. O. Lundy of El Campo, Texas, was his name—a man of truth, an example of integrity and godliness.

My younger daughter Colleen and I were traveling through Texas in the fall of 1987. We decided to take a few blue highways and drive through my hometown. I had not returned there for over thirty years. We drove into El Campo and finally located my grandparents' home. Almost immediately after parking in front of that place where my grandparents lived many years earlier, my tears began to flow. And so did Colleen's. She has heard me speak often of his influence on my life. She read my mind. I looked at an old, stately house where there once lived a great gentleman. What I remember most is the love he demonstrated as he took a little grandson on his knee and spoke kindly to him and modeled righteousness and shaped his thinking. Naturally, neither he nor I had any idea where my future would lead me. As she and I sat out front, looking at the windows and the front door and the porch and the little walkway, I was overwhelmed with gratitude. I remembered the truth, and I remembered the one from whom I had learned the truth.

Who was it with you? Whom could you name? Were you blessed with parents who loved God? Are you blessed with grandparents like that? Was it a godly, faithful pastor? Don't let the speed of today cause you to treat the depth of your past lightly. Return to the truth of your past. Review those lives and those events. Remember them, renew them, rely on them, then relay the truth on to your children. It will hold you fast through the turmoil of the future. When shallow personalities come and go and you are tempted to be swept off your feet, when hard times come and almost level you, go back to your roots and find spiritual solidity there.

If your past, like Timothy's, includes a godly heritage, you have been wonderfully blessed. The severity and depravity of these last days will not overwhelm you. You will find strength and stability in the midst of the storm. And you will be better equipped to minister in the last days.

1.   How can we the church, Christ's representative on earth, follow Paul's directive to face realistically the savage times in which we live and still remain positive in our attitude and outlook? Take a moment to write down two or three timeless, biblical principles that can help you and your family maintain balance and perspective in this often crazed era in which we live. Discuss these with your family, your Bible study group, or a close Christian friend.

2.   Who are your models in the Christian life? Can you name one or two—perhaps visualizing their faces? Can you hear their encouraging voices cheering you on from the grandstands (Hebrews 12:1–2), urging you to endure and remain faithful? If you have such models, take time to consider them more frequently. Ask yourself how they might respond in some of the difficult circumstances in which you may find yourself. What might their counsel be? Ask the Lord to help you emulate their example—and don't be reluctant to speak of that example to your family and friends. As one of my mentors used to say, "If we all talked about our heroes, we would have more heroes to talk about."

3.   Speaking of worthy models, how long has it been since you have read the biography of an exemplary Christian man or woman? Take time this week to peruse the biography shelf of your local Christian bookstore and make what could be a life-changing purchase.

"Stayin' Ready 'til Quittin' Time"

After I graduated from high school, I worked in a machine shop in Houston's industrial district for four-and-a-half years. I was not only learning the machinist trade as an apprentice, I was also going to night school at the University of Houston. My father was from the old school of thought; he believed I should not only get a good education but also learn a trade so I would have something to fall back on if some career I followed ever fell through. I followed his advice and have never regretted it.

I have many great memories of those years in that machine shop. I learned a lot of valuable lessons while working with my hands—one of them being a true appreciation for the blue-collar world. I have no trouble understanding what that life is like, its pressures and frustrations as well as its benefits and feelings of accomplishment.

I often recall several unforgettable characters I met during those days. What fun we had together! One of them was a fellow I'll call Tex. He and I worked alongside each other on second shift for several months.

Tex had spent most of his adult life operating a turret lathe in the same shop. He was your typical machinist. He wore a little gray-and-white striped cap—always greasy—and overalls that needed an oil change. And, of course, he chewed tobacco, which meant he spit a lot. He would keep his tobacco pouch open in his right hip pocket, and as he ran his lathe, he would reach back, grab a fistful of that stringy stuff, cram it into his mouth, then chew on it for an hour or so. That entire procedure occurred without his eyes ever leaving his work on the lathe. Tex would easily chew his way through several pouches a week.

One hot, sticky night as I was working behind Tex on a similar lathe, I noticed that a Texas-size cricket hopped unassumingly through the door onto the floor of our shop. As I studied the little critter, I noticed that the color of the cricket was almost identical to the color of the tobacco in Tex's pouch. So, without Tex knowing it, I strolled over and stepped on Jiminy, quickly putting him out of his misery. I then plucked the head off the little guy, reached over and placed him very gently on the top of the open tobacco pouch sticking out of Tex's pocket. I then quietly strolled back to my lathe and waited . . . and watched.

After a while he needed to replenish his chaw, so he reached back and grabbed a fresh fistful. In went the cricket along with a jaw full of tobacco. To this day Tex has no idea what he chewed that night. I can still remember watching him spit wings and legs and body parts for the next hour or so. It was hilarious!

When you work in a machine shop, your life revolves around a whistle. After punching the clock when you arrive, your work begins with a whistle. As lunchtime arrives, it is announced by the same shrill sound. When your shift ends, there is yet another blast.

Shoptalk for that final whistle is "quittin' time."

Tex had worked so long in a machine shop, he had kind of an invisible sensor down inside. He seldom had to look at the clock. Somehow he always knew when it was getting close to that last whistle. I cannot recall his ever being caught short. Without fail, Tex was all washed up and ready to punch out a couple of minutes before the whistle blew.

On one occasion I said to him, "Well, Tex, it's about time to start gettin' ready for quittin' time."

I will never forget his response. In that slow Texas drawl, he said, "Listen, boy . . . I stay ready to keep from gettin' ready for quittin' time." It was his way of saying, "That final whistle won't ever catch me unaware."

Many long years have passed since I worked with Tex, but his answer has stuck in my mind when I think of that last sound before our Lord comes back. It won't be from a whistle in a machine shop, but with other sounds far more earsplitting. In fact, Scripture says,

> The Lord Himself will descend from heaven with a **shout** . . .
> (1 Thessalonians 4:16).

The word means "an outcry." I don't know if it will be the Lord Himself or someone near Him, but there will be a loud outcry from heaven. And that's not all. There will also be—

> . . . the voice of the archangel, and with the trumpet of God
> (v. 16).

And then—

> . . . the dead in Christ shall rise first. Then we who are alive and remain shall be caught up together with them in the clouds to meet the Lord in the air, and thus we shall always be with the Lord. Therefore comfort one another with these words (1 Thessalonians 4:16–17).

Are you "stayin' ready 'til quittin' time"? There are times I wonder how many will be caught off guard. Do thoughts ever come to your mind, as you are busily engaged in your daily grind, like, "Say, it may happen today. It could be right after supper."? Or, "He may return before bedtime tonight." Let me tell you when most of us think such a thought: when we have to pay our taxes! That's when we all wish He would come quickly. But, seriously, does it ever flash through your head, "Today could be my last day on earth. He could split the heavens today and shout 'It's quittin' time!'"?

Some folks would have to admit that thought never crosses their minds. I mean, *never*, even though while He was still on earth, our Lord gave numerous predictions about His coming back.

A FEW PREDICTIONS FROM JESUS' LIFE

Let's look at several. I've chosen one from each of the four Gospels.

Periodically, during the ministry of Christ, He spoke of this. Each time He mentioned His certain return, His words seemed like a wake-up call in the early morning hours.

> *Therefore be on the alert, for you do not know which day your Lord is coming. But be sure of this, that if the head of the house had known at what time of the night the thief was coming, he would have been on the alert and would not have allowed his house to be broken into* (Matthew 24:42–43).

How practical! If you have ever been gone overnight and had your home broken into by a burglar, or if your place of business has ever been robbed in the middle of the night, you know that the thief was successful because his entrance was unexpected and his exit undetected. That's Jesus' point here. "My coming will be like a thief in the night. When you least expect it, I'll come." He then applies this to His return:

> *For this reason you be ready too; for the Son of Man is coming at an hour when you do not think He will* (v. 44).

I once read about an armored car that was left unattended for less than five minutes. It had over a million dollars in it. During those unattended moments, thieves came and robbed it. They knew just when to come and how to leave so that no one had any idea they were there—until it was too late.

We find similar words about the same event in Mark's Gospel. Again, Jesus is speaking:

*Take heed, keep on the alert; for you do not know when the
appointed time is. It is like a man, away on a journey, who
upon leaving his house and putting his slaves in charge, assign-
ing to each one his task, also commanded the doorkeeper to stay
on the alert. Therefore, be on the alert—for you do not know
when the master of the house is coming, whether in the evening,
at midnight, at cockcrowing, or in the morning—lest he come
suddenly and find you asleep. And what I say to you I say to
all, "Be on the alert!"* (13:33–37).

You and I are intrigued with His reference to "cockcrowing,"
aren't we? It calls for an explanation. Our nights are not divided
as they were in Jesus' time. First-century nights were divided into
watches—four three-hour watches, to be exact. The first watch
began at sundown, around 6:00 P.M., and ended at 9:00 P.M. The
second watch continued from 9:00 P.M. until 12:00 midnight. And
the third watch occurred from 12:00 midnight to 3:00 in the
morning.

There was a familiar Latin term used to describe the end of
the third watch, *gallicinium*. It meant "cockcrowing." I suppose
the name was derived from some early-rising rooster that would
stretch his neck and sound his first call around three in the morning. Christ could come then! Or, says our Lord, He may come at
dawn, in the misty morning hour around sunrise. The point is:
anytime.

Dr. Luke records similar words. The more we read these repeated words of Jesus, the more assured we become: Not only is He
coming back . . . we must be ready.

*Be on guard, that your hearts may not be weighted down with
dissipation and drunkenness and the worries of life, and that
day come on you suddenly like a trap* (Luke 21:34).

How different! Matthew used the analogy of a thief, but now
Luke mentions a trap. If you are trapped in an embarrassing setting, full of worry, or in a drunken state or a dissipating
lifestyle—as some people will be—you won't be ready for quittin'

time. His warning is clear: Don't be caught short lest you be trapped at His coming.

> *For it will come upon all those who dwell on the face of all the earth. But keep on the alert at all times, praying in order that you may have strength to escape all these things that are about to take place, and to stand before the Son of Man* (vv. 35–36).

Many years later, at the end of the first century, John recorded his observations and thoughts. Among John's most significant contributions were his writings of the Upper Room discourse. Jesus is with His Twelve the night before He is taken under arrest and goes to the cross. While there, He abruptly unveils the truth of His impending death. It catches the disciples off guard. They became visibly shaken, and understandably so. Had we been among His disciples, we, too, would have expected Him to live forever, establish His kingdom, and take us with Him as He became the King of kings and Lord of lords, ruling over the whole earth.

But suddenly He introduces a change in the game plan—the Cross. Full of turmoil, doubt, and fear, the disciples stared in stunned amazement as He spoke of His imminent death. That explains why He said what He did to them regarding His return.

> *Let not your heart be troubled; believe in God, believe also in Me. In My Father's house are many dwelling places; if it were not so, I would have told you; for I go to prepare a place for you. And if I go and prepare a place for you, I will come again, and receive you to Myself; that where I am, there you may be also* (John 14:1–3).

To those anxious disciples He gave an unconditional promise. He doesn't say, "If you're expecting Me, I'll come back." He doesn't even say, "If you're walking with Me, I'll come back." No, His promise is absolutely unconditional. "I am going to prepare a place . . . I will return . . . I will receive you . . . you will be with Me." His return was no guesswork . . . it would occur!

No doubt, they wondered what to expect in the meanwhile. Within minutes He covered that base.

These things I have spoken to you, that in Me you may have peace. In the world you have tribulation, but take courage; I have overcome the world (John 16:33).

"I have left heaven. I have begun My ministry on this earth. I have been sustained by God's power. I will soon complete My mission. I must go to the cross to pay the penalty for sins. I will come out of the grave victorious. I will ascend to the Father. And I will come again at His appointed time." In the meantime, He challenged them to be alert. "Stay ready 'til quittin' time." While awaiting His return, they were sure to face affliction and tribulation.

We have been building toward this subject since we began this book together, haven't we? We have been thinking about the church—its purpose, objectives, style, and the changes that will occur during these last days. In the previous chapter we addressed a couple of the guidelines we should follow in light of the days of difficulty that we must endure. It might help to think of them as "survival techniques." How do we make it? Since the world is going to make times hard for us, how can we live courageously, knowing that He has overcome the world? What are we in the church to do?

Clearly, Christ is going to return. Our question is this: How can we best "stay ready 'til quittin' time"?

SPECIFIC PRINCIPLES FROM PAUL'S PEN

Turn again to those last words Paul wrote in the second letter to Timothy. He penned these words a little past A.D. 60. He has come to the end of his life, which prompts him to describe life at the end of time. As we saw in the previous chapter, times will only get worse. Paul pulls no punches as he writes his friend Timothy and says, "We're in for difficult times . . . savage, in fact." How can we stay ready for the finale? How can we be sure that the curtain's closing will not take us by surprise or find us finishing poorly? What are we to do?

As I mentioned earlier there are four principles to follow. They are set forth in the third and fourth chapters of 2 Timothy. You may remember the first: *Follow the model of the faithful.*

> *But you followed my teaching, conduct, purpose, faith, patience, love, perseverance, persecutions, and sufferings, such as happened to me at Antioch, at Iconium and at Lystra; what persecutions I endured, and out of them all the Lord delivered me! And indeed, all who desire to live godly in Christ Jesus will be persecuted* (2 Timothy 3:10–12).

There is nothing more encouraging or more motivating than a model to keep us going.

I don't know if you've read of the five-hundred-mile dogsled race over a part of Minnesota. Have you kept up on that? The same lady who won in 1987 also won in 1988. We're talking a pioneer woman! She pressed on through bitter cold, the howling winds of a blizzard, dark nights, and exhausting days, as her well-trained huskies pulled her sled over those hundreds of miles from the start to the finish of the race. The dogs were fitted with little socks over their paws since the ice resembles sandpaper after so many miles. It can literally rip the pads off their feet. Though strong and in great condition, the struggling animals with those little socks on their feet barked, pulled, and pressed on in spite of the odds.

After the race she was interviewed and asked, "How did you do it?"

"Well," she said, "I just remembered that others have done it before me, so I can do it, too."

If that wasn't enough, when I shared that story recently, I had a fellow say to me, "Did you know there is an eleven-hundred-mile race from Anchorage to Nome?" He then informed me that the same woman, Susan Butcher, has won that race three times in a row! Is that unbelievable? Ten to twelve days in the middle of nowhere. Maddening monotony. Strain beyond belief. How does she do it? I can tell you part of the answer . . . she remembers someone else did it before her. That assures her that she can do it too.

The same works today. By following the model of those who have gone before us, we can do more than survive. We can overcome! That is how composers of music stay at the task of writing music. That is how people exist through torturous conditions as prisoners of war. That is how surgeons continue to push on through the night hours in emergency surgery. That is how athletes set new records. There have been models who have done it before.

The same works in the spiritual life. That is why Paul tells Timothy to follow the model of his faithful mother and grandmother . . . and Paul's own example as well.

What a rich heritage! Timothy had deep roots to sustain him through dry and unfruitful days.

Remember the second principle? *Return to the truth of your past.* As you follow the model of the faithful, go back to the things you learned from your mother, the truth you gleaned from your grandmother, and your early years at the feet of a mentor in the classroom. Go back to those truths that stabilized you when you put down your spiritual roots.

I spent a few hours in Chicago several years ago, recording an interview with *Leadership* magazine. There were four of us who had been invited from various sections of the country to be interviewed. I'll never forget a comment from one of the men who holds a responsible position in a sizable denomination. He has his finger on the pulse of the church at large. He said something like this:

> We have discovered that those who make the best church leaders, those who hold important and responsible positions over vast numbers of people, are almost without exception people who have deep, longstanding roots in the faith. Very few of them were saved at, say, age 35 or 40, and are now leading a large segment of God's family. Almost without exception, those who have been promot-

ed to places of great responsibility can look back to godly parents and even grandparents who walked with God. And from them they learned, even from early childhood, the value of the church, the significance of the Scriptures.[25]

Don't misread that statement. It doesn't mean if you were saved later in life you will never be given a place of great responsibility. As Christians, all of us have great responsibilities. It's just interesting that the majority of those who are in high-profile leadership positions in the church today heard the truth early in life. They had solid Christian roots. If that was your experience, it is a great time to give thanks for the kind of faith you drew from them.

And notice in verse 15 that he has in mind,

> . . . *the sacred writings which are able to give you wisdom*. . . .

What are the sacred writings? The next verse gives the answer:

> *All Scripture is inspired by God* . . . (v. 16).

Beautiful word—inspired. *Theos* (God), plus *pneuma* (breath)—*theopneustos* is the Greek word . . . "God-breathed." All Scripture in its original form has been breathed out by God so that a writer, under the controlling power of the Spirit of God, wrote the Scriptures precisely as God would have written them. He did this without error, down to the very terms used, including the order of the terms in which they were written, with the result that God's very word was miraculously recorded. "All of that was 'God-breathed,' Timothy."

But that isn't where it ends. It has been preserved in the pages of our Bibles so that as a result of reading and absorbing the Scriptures, we find them

> . . . *profitable for teaching, for reproof, for correction, for training in righteousness* . . . (v. 16).

Isn't that a grand set of benefits? As important as it may be, great parenting is not an absolute prerequisite for spiritual growth or involvement in church leadership. God has given each of us the

Bible in our tongue, with the promise that it is profitable for teaching, for reproof, for correction, and for training in righteousness. Each one of us has the potential to become, like Timothy, a person who is adequate, mature, equipped for every good work. God's truth has been deposited into our reservoir. All this explains how Paul can say to his friend Timothy, "In the hard times draw upon the Scriptures."

Unfortunately, there is a chapter break in our Bibles between 2 Timothy 3:17 and 2 Timothy 4:1 which interrupts the flow of thought. Ignore it. Simply consider the new chapter as a continuation of the same theme.

> *I solemnly charge you in the presence of God and of Christ Jesus, who is to judge the living and the dead, and by His appearing and His kingdom* (v. 1).

As he mentions our Lord's judging the living and the dead, Paul is reminding Timothy of Christ's return. "Quittin' time" is a sure fact. "Until He comes back, Timothy . . ."

> *Preach the word; be ready in season and out of season; reprove, rebuke, exhort, with great patience and instruction* (v. 2).

This statement brings us to the third "survival" principle: *Proclaim the message of Christ.* Timothy has been called to be a preacher. It makes sense that he proclaimed Christ. You may not be a preacher, but the principle *still* applies. In light of these difficult days, all of us must heed the same command.

As I think about Paul's instruction, I find three ingredients. First, I find *urgency.* Be ready. "Stay ready to keep from gettin' ready!" Be ready with the right message at all times.

Second, I find *consistency.* "Be ready in season and out of season." Let's make a list.

- When it is convenient. When it is inconvenient.

- When others are open. When others are closed.

- When you're feeling good or you're feeling poorly.

- Whether you're young or old.

- Whether early or late.

- Whether it is cold and windy or hot and humid.

- Whether you're in public or private, at home or in a strange place.

- When you're appreciated or when you're resented.

- When you're asked about it or when you're not asked about it.

In season, out of season . . . that's Paul's way of saying that the secret is consistency. What an effective force are those who know the truth and consistently live it out and share it. When we do, the Scriptures become absorbed into our very being.

Spurgeon put it this way:

It is blessed to eat into the very soul of the Bible, until, at last, you come to talk in scriptural language, and your spirit is flavored with the words of the Lord, so that your blood is *Bibline* and the very essence of the Bible flows from you.[26]

Third, I find *simplicity*. Isn't it beautiful? There is nothing sophisticated about Paul's exhortation. No theories, no complex opinions. "Just take the body of truth that I have given and declare it. Since you have the Scriptures, you have all the groceries you need for folks who are hungry." God's Word contains sufficient comfort, hope, and encouragement to help the lonely and the hurting. Our need is to keep it simple. There is something quietly motivating about simplicity.

In one of my earlier books I cited a simple note emerging from the black and brutal days of the Civil War. The communication came from a battle-weary President Lincoln to his general, Ulysses S. Grant. Only three lines, yet it was the written missile that ended the war. The date and the time appeared at the top:

> April 7, 1865
> 11 o'clock a.m.
>
> General Sheridan says, "If the thing is pressed, I think that Lee will surrender."
>
> Let the thing be pressed.
>
> A. Lincoln[27]

Grant got the message and acted upon it. He pressed it. Two days later at Appomattox courthouse, Robert E. Lee surrendered. The thing was pressed, and the bloodiest war in American history ended. Simplicity is indeed powerful.

You want to stay ready 'til quittin' time?

- Follow the model of the faithful.

- Return to the truth of your past.

- Proclaim the message of Christ.

There is a final principle: *Maintain an exemplary life.*

For the time will come when they will not endure sound doctrine; but wanting to have their ears tickled, they will accumulate for themselves teachers in accordance to their own desires; and will turn away their ears from the truth, and will turn aside to myths. But you, be sober in all things, endure hardship, do the work of an evangelist, fulfill your ministry (vv. 3–5).

There will always be teachers who tickle people's fancy, telling them what they want to hear rather than what they *ought* to hear. Count on it—the closer we get to the Savior's return, the more these ear-ticklers will proliferate. How are we to counteract that?

The answer appears in four staccato commands in verse 5:

- Be sober in all things.
- Endure hardship.
- Do the work of an evangelist.
- Fulfill your ministry.

Because people are unstable and forever on a search for cute fads and clever novelties, we are to steer clear of all that nonsense, staying calm and steady. Once again, John Stott's words are worth repeating:

> When men and women get intoxicated with heady heresies and sparkling novelties [we] must keep calm and sane.

Want a tip for finding the right church? Look for the ministry that is calm and sane. Stay away from those who highlight all the flash-in-the-pan fads, the cutesy, the clever.

And when the going gets rougher, "endure hardship." In today's terms, gut it out. Stay at it. But don't get sour and cranky. Just keep on presenting Christ. Realizing that the phony and the false will be on the increase, live the truth, walk your talk. By doing that you "fulfill your ministry."

TIMELESS FACTS THAT MAINTAIN OUR READINESS

For I am already being poured out as a drink offering, and the time of my departure has come. I have fought the good fight, I have finished the course, I have kept the faith; in the future there is laid up for me the crown of righteousness, which the Lord, the righteous Judge, will award to me on that day; and not only to me, but also to all who have loved His appearing (vv. 6–8).

How can a Christian stay ready 'til quittin' time? How can we keep from being caught up short? How can I guarantee that my life won't be surprised to hear that last shout, the voice, and the trumpet blast from heaven? Three suggestions emerge from Paul's words.

First: *Consider your life an offering to God rather than a monument to men*. Paul writes of being poured out as an offering. That is a vivid word picture worth emulating. Think of yourself as the sacrifice. Don't work on your image, work on your offering. Consider your life as little more than an offering poured out to God, rather than a polished monument for men to admire.

Second: *Remember that finishing well is the final proof that the truth works*. I find that woven into the words of verse 7:

> *I have fought the good fight, I have finished the course, I have kept the faith.*

Don't you admire people who finish? Sometimes just finishing is as impressive as winning. Remember the Olympics of 1984? If you do, you can never forget the lady who ran that marathon and finally made it back to the stadium. Remember her? She was struggling to stay on her feet . . . I mean, my family and I were watching her on television and urging, "Come on. Come on! Don't stop!" As she was trying to focus on the tape, she stumbled and fell. And we yelled all the more, "Get up! Get up!" She did. She finally made it across the tape. She didn't win anything. In fact, she was so late it was already a done deal. For all practical purposes, the race had ended. But *she finished*. When she finally crossed over, I don't know about your family, but ours applauded and shouted in unison, "ALL RIGHT!" You'd have thought it was our godmother crossing that line! Glory . . . she finished!

Plan now to finish what you have begun. It will help when the race seems extra long.

Paul concludes:

> *In the future there is laid up for me the crown of righteousness, which the Lord, the righteous Judge, will award to me on that day; and not only to me, but also to all who have loved His appearing* (v. 8).

Third: *Fix your eyes on the rewards of heaven rather than the allurements of earth*. There is a crown coming. So much of life depends upon the focus of our eyes, doesn't it? It recently occurred to me that as valuable as my eyes may be, they need my mind before they can do the work they must do. My eyeballs enable me to see. I am able to see *with* my eyes. But I need to use my mind to see *through* things.

Illustration: Lot and Abraham. Back in the Genesis account, uncle Abraham and nephew Lot are living together. God prospers their livestock so abundantly that they cannot stay on the same ranch. So Abraham graciously says to his nephew, "Look, my son, decide where you wish to live. You pick it out. And wherever you and your family prefer to live, take your goods and your livestock and move. I'll take whatever's left."

And Lot?

And Lot lifted up his eyes and saw all the valley of the Jordan, that it was well watered everywhere . . . (Genesis 13:10).

He saw *with* his eyes how beautiful an area, how comfortable—but he failed to see *through* it. He didn't stop to think, "This wicked place is Sodom. And Gomorrah is just as bad. Perversion is rampant. This area and these people will take their toll on my family." Like many, he saw with his eyes, but failed to see through. Remember that. As you use your eyes to focus on the heavenly rewards, keep your mind alert so you can see through this earth's allurements.

Malcolm Muggeridge has frequently quoted the couplet from William Blake:

> *This Life's dim Windows of the Soul*
> *Distort the Heavens from Pole to Pole.*
> *And lead you to Believe a Lie*
> *When you see with not thro the Eye.*[28]

If we are committed to "stayin' ready 'til quittin' time," the plan isn't all that complicated. We will need to follow the model of the faithful. We will need to return to the truth of the past. As His Bride, we must proclaim the message of Christ. And in the process, we dare not fail to maintain an exemplary life.

The unbroken gold bands exchanged at weddings symbolize that two will be committed to one another—eternally. Or in the words of this chapter, 'til quittin' time. Christ has pledged Himself to His Bride forever. Have we done the same to Him? Will we—*forever?*

1. Maybe today. Maybe tonight. Do those thoughts ever pass through your mind as your feet first hit the floor in the morning or as you fall back on your pillow at night? It may be a long while since you've done any serious reflection about our Lord's imminent return. Take some index cards and jot down several of the extended Scripture passages we've looked at in this chapter. Carry them with you for a week or two, or post them where you will be able to see them through the day. Let the truth of those words saturate your mind and heart as you read them again and again.

2. Go back to the list on pages 153–54 that comes under the words "Be ready in season and out of season." Underneath that sentence, I have listed nine statements beginning with the words "When" or "Whether." On a piece of paper, try to tie each of those situations with real people, real places, and real circumstances from your own life. Let this exercise begin to paint a picture of what a consistent witness for Christ would actually look like in your life.

3. Have you ever memorized a simple gospel presentation—one that you know so well you could use it any time under any circumstances? What a demonstration of Who in this life in the most important to you, so important that you want to tell others about how you got to know Him! Take a look at several possibilities (these could include "The Four Spiritual Laws," from Campus Crusade; "The Bridge," from the Navigators; or "Steps to Peace with God," by the Billy Graham organization). Firm up this presentation in your head, and then watch for opportunities to give it away—in season and out of season!

THE VALUE OF INTEGRITY

Tuesday dawned cold at the launch site.

Yet some distance away from Cape Canaveral on that icy morning, the air was filled with heated debate.

Unknown to the rest of the nation, a war of words raged behind the scenes. The verbal battle was between clear-thinking engineers and technicians who were saying "No" on one side of the disagreement and influential executives and image-conscious bureaucrats who were saying "Yes" on the other. The argument was over whether the space shuttle *Challenger* should be launched that morning . . . January 28, 1986.

Against the strong advice of experts who knew the temperature had dropped too low for the launch to be considered safe, the countdown continued right up to lift-off.

Seventy seconds later—to the horror of a nation—the *Challenger's* crew of seven perished in a mammoth explosion. Debris rained into the sea for a full hour.

Technicians pinpointed the cause of the explosion as a faulty seal that allowed the volatile fuel to leak and ignite.

That was the technical explanation. The real reason for *Challenger's* demise went deeper than the breakdown of a faulty O-ring. It began with a breakdown of integrity, both in the construction of the shuttle and in the character of those who refused to heed the warnings.

A CRISIS OF INTEGRITY

This will not be an easy chapter to write. It took me over three years to prepare it in my mind. The events that have led to my putting these thoughts into print have been both heartbreaking and scandalous. They have left a black eye on the face of Uncle Sam and, even worse, they have crippled the church of Jesus Christ.

What has occurred is nothing less than an integrity crisis. It has not happened overnight. Like erosion, its onslaught has been slow and sinister.

The crisis has spread to our highways, which have become scenes of slaughter. Despite gallant efforts by volunteer organizations, a costly advertisement campaign, and stricter judicial punishments, drunk and/or drugged drivers continue to get behind the wheel and murder innocent victims. It is now well documented that at least half of all traffic deaths are caused by those guilty of substance abuse. Such people lack the integrity it takes to say no to irresponsible driving.

Acquired Immune Deficiency Syndrome (AIDS)—words we never heard of fifteen years ago—is now front-page news. The implications are unfathomable. In a matter of months a 220-pound athlete can be reduced to a 90-pound spectator, ultimately becoming an entry on the obituary column. If the Surgeon General's estimate is correct, this lapse-in-integrity disease will someday fill pages of our metropolitan newspapers. As of July 1994, a total of 2.1 million Americans already have AIDS and another 13 million have the pre-AIDS HIV. I did a quick calculation of that figure and discovered that if you printed two names per line, that many fatalities would require more than eighty pages of an average-size newspaper . . . listing top to bottom, six columns across, excluding all headlines, pictures, and advertisements. That, my friend, is an epidemic.

The military service once bragged about its integrity. My own particular branch, the U.S. Marines, held high its motto, *Semper Fidelis*. No longer, in the minds of the public. Thanks to a sex-for-spying scandal in Moscow, those once-proud leathernecks now must face the embarrassment of an editorial cartoonist whose caption "*Semper Infidelis*" said it all. Marine guards jettisoned integrity as they escorted Soviet agents into the most sensitive chambers of the consulate in Moscow—including the "secure" top-secret communications center. Entire lists of secret agents were revealed, leaving them threatened by exposure. The repeated transmission of secret codes and documents immobilized future defense plans.

What caused the Marines to do that? Were they forced at gunpoint? Was it brainwashing or torture? Nuclear blackmail? No. It was sexual lust . . . a weakening of moral integrity.

The political arena, once a place of great admiration and high-level trust, is now a study in compromise. Scandals abound. Everything from plagiarism to alcoholism, from deception to corruption, from sexual favors to financial payoffs continue to emerge. Again, integrity is conspicuous by its absence.

As difficult as it is for me to include this final category, I cannot omit it. I am referring to the dreadful track record of so many religious leaders, especially in the past decade. There have always been a few Elmer Gantry types, I realize, but I cannot recall a time in modern church history when the number of defectors has been so high or the extent of their questionable or shameful activities so bold. To rehearse each incident is both needless and counterproductive, but to remind ourselves of the consequences is essential.

Public opinion of religious workers is at an all-time low. Pollster George Gallup, Jr. recently told a group of Christian fundraisers that "forty-two percent of Americans doubted the honesty of some, if not most, appeals for religious donations."[29] What they really doubt is our integrity.

INTEGRITY: THERE IS NO SUBSTITUTE

Before proceeding, we need to define the term. Scripturally, integrity is from a Hebrew word that means "whole, sound, unimpaired." Webster states that integrity means "an unimpaired condition: soundness." Amplifying the meaning, he goes on to include "adherence to a code of moral, artistic, or other values . . . the quality or state of being complete or undivided." When one has integrity there is an absence of hypocrisy. He or she is personally reliable, financially accountable, and privately clean . . . innocent of impure motives.

> There is a certain blend of courage . . . character, and principle which has no satisfactory dictionary name but has been called different things at different times in different countries. Our American name for it is "guts."[30]

Integrity is not only the way one thinks but even more the way one acts. As Ted Engstrom declares, "Integrity is doing what you said you would do."[31] It is as basic as keeping your word, fulfilling your promise. For example:

- You told the Lord you would give Him all the glory.

- You promised you would be faithful to your mate.

- You declared that your expenses amounted to a certain figure.

- You promised your son you would play ball this afternoon.

- You told your publisher he would have the manuscript by March 20.

- You assured your roommate you would carry out

your end of the load.

- You promised at your ordination that you would be true to your calling.

- You signed a contract that committed you to specific things.

- You told your neighbor you would bring back the tool you borrowed.

- You swore to tell the truth when you took the stand.

- You stated you would pray or return a phone call or pay your bill or show up at 6:30 . . . etc.

No reason to complicate matters or search for excuses. Doing what you said you would do is simply an issue of integrity. There is no substitute for having the *guts* to keep your word.

Integrity evidences itself in ethical soundness, intellectual veracity, and moral excellence. It keeps us from fearing the white light of close examination and from resisting the scrutiny of accountability. It is honesty at all cost . . . rocklike character that won't crack when standing alone or crumble when pressure mounts.

INTEGRITY IN SCRIPTURE

Integrity appears no less than sixteen times in Scripture, every time in the Old Testament. For example, the psalmist, while under the gun, prayed, "Vindicate me, O LORD, according to . . . my integrity" (7:8). And, again, when tempted: "Let integrity and uprightness preserve me" (25:21). When looking for a new king to replace Saul, God pursued a young man who had integrity. I love the description of the selection process recorded in Psalm 78:

> *He also chose David His servant, and took him from the sheep-folds; from the care of the ewes with suckling lambs He brought him, to shepherd Jacob His people, and Israel His inheritance.*

So he shepherded them according to the integrity of his heart, and guided them with his skillful hands (vv. 70–72).

Wise Solomon writes of how a father's thumbprint of integrity marks his children for good:

A righteous man who walks in his integrity—how blessed are his sons after him (Proverbs 20:7).

Biblical characters often display integrity, without the word itself being used. Joseph, while the trusted house servant of Potiphar, was the target of Mrs. Potiphar's seduction. You owe it to yourself to read the account in Genesis 39. Scripture presents in vivid color her lurid and frequent attempts to get Joseph into her bed. You can almost feel the temptress's arms around you, smell the fragrance of her perfume. The lights are low, the sheets are satin, the wine is poured, soft music plays in the background, they are alone . . . and she wants him!

But the most beautiful part of the story is Joseph's integrity. Out of devotion to his God and loyalty to his master (her husband), the man literally runs from her arms. From the way the story reads, he refused even to flirt with the idea of yielding. He gave her no come-on signals . . . not even subtle ones. The man had moral guts, rare in our day of unbridled affairs.

Other examples? Consider Elijah. Armed with the message of God, he stood toe-to-toe with Ahab and Jezebel, warning them of approaching judgment (1 Kings 17:1). I think of Nathan, the unintimidated prophet who had the guts to look adulterous David in the eye and say, "You are the man!" (2 Samuel 12:1–12). Or John the Baptizer, who attracted a crowd into the wilderness, yet never used the opportunity to build a following around himself. He was a preacher who willingly lost his congregation to Another, all the while modeling his humble statement of integrity, "He must increase, but I must decrease" (John 3:30). I'm reminded of Stephen, whose bold witness for Christ so incited the hostility of the Jewish Sanhedrin, they stoned him to death. To the very end he spoke the truth without wavering (Acts 6:8–7:60) . . . which may have been the first time Saul of Tarsus ever heard the gospel (Acts 7:58).

I find it encouraging that great people of integrity mentioned in the Bible can be found in every stratum of society . . . at any financial level, filling every conceivable role or place of occupation, living in places of beauty or poverty, representing single and married alike. Hebrews 11 sets forth a list of such, including one man or woman after another under the heading, "people of faith." Though they lived exemplary (not perfect) lives, their earthly fate was anything but pleasant and rewarding.

> *And what more shall I say? For time will fail me if I tell of Gideon, Barak, Samson, Jephthah, of David and Samuel and the prophets, who by faith conquered kingdoms, performed acts of righteousness, obtained promises, shut the mouths of lions, quenched the power of fire, escaped the edge of the sword, from weakness were made strong, became mighty in war, put foreign armies to flight. Women received back their dead by resurrection; and others were tortured, not accepting their release, in order that they might obtain a better resurrection; and others experienced mockings and scourgings, yes, also chains and imprisonment. They were stoned, they were sawn in two, they were tempted, they were put to death with the sword; they went about in sheepskins, in goat-skins, being destitute, afflicted, illtreated (men of whom the world was not worthy), wandering in deserts and mountains and caves and holes in the ground (vv. 32–38).*

Please don't misunderstand. Having integrity isn't usually some high-profile, lay-down-your-life-as-a-martyr issue. More often than not it is in the quiet, unnoticed, unapplauded realms of life that one demonstrates integrity . . . within the walls of one's own home . . . in the secret chambers of one's own heart.

DANIEL: A CLASSIC CASE FOR INTEGRITY

A man in the Bible whose middle name could have been Integrity stood head and shoulders above his peers. His sixty-two-year-old superior, King Darius, had no idea how corrupt Daniel's colleagues were. He admired Daniel, however, and made plans to promote him over all the rest. Here is a quick summary of the story as it unfolded centuries ago:

> *It seemed good to Darius to appoint 120 satraps over the kingdom, that they should be in charge of the whole kingdom, and over them three commissioners (of whom Daniel was one), that these satraps might be accountable to them, and that the king might not suffer loss. Then this Daniel began distinguishing himself among the commissioners and satraps because he possessed an extraordinary spirit, and the king planned to appoint him over the entire kingdom (Daniel 6:1–3).*

Generally speaking, there are two kinds of tests in life: adversity and prosperity. Of the two, the latter is the more difficult. When adversity strikes, things get simple; survival is the goal. It is a test on maintaining the basics of food, clothing, and shelter. But when prosperity comes, watch out! Things get complicated. All kinds of subtle temptations arrive, pleading for satisfaction. It is then that one's integrity is put to the test.

That is where Daniel was: trusted, successful, on the verge of a promotion. But none of the above caused him to compromise his integrity even slightly. In spite of his spotless character, the pressure mounted. His peers, no doubt out of jealously, decided to find some dirt in his life in order to report it to the king.

> *Then the commissioners and satraps began trying to find a ground of accusation against Daniel in regard to government affairs; but they could find no ground of accusation or evidence of corruption, inasmuch as he was faithful, and no negligence or corruption was to be found in him (v. 4).*

We would say they "tailed" him. They spied on him, talked with others about him, watched him, and rifled through his files. They were determined to find an accusation against him. They found ZERO. No hanky-panky. No secret funds. No fraud. No hushed cover-ups. No payoffs. Not a hint of corruption. The man was squeaky clean. *What an example of integrity!* How we need to model it, regardless of the mediocrity around us. In every area of life! We have existed so long without it, we no longer expect to find it—except perhaps in a few isolated realms of society. But integrity fits where it is found.

> The society which scorns excellence in plumbing because plumbing is a humble activity and tolerates shoddiness in philosophy because it is an exalted activity will have neither good plumbing nor good philosophy. Neither its pipes nor its theories will hold water.[32]

Having integrity won't always win friends. As in Daniel's case, others will often turn up the heat. The world system is so saturated with compromise and corruption, whoever determines to live above all that will be a silent reproof to those who don't. A few may admire you for it, more will resent you. Be ready for their assault. They will stop at nothing to make life miserable for you—even if it means bending the truth to fit their scheme.

That is precisely what happened to Daniel. As a matter of fact, *that* is how he wound up in the lions' den.

> *Then these men said, "We shall not find any ground of accusation against this Daniel unless we find it against him with regard to the law of his God." Then these commissioners and satraps came by agreement to the king and spoke to him as follows: "King Darius, live forever! All the commissioners of the kingdom, the prefects and the satraps, the high officials and the governors have consulted together that the king should establish a statute and enforce an injunction that anyone who makes a petition to any god or man besides you, O king, for thirty days, shall be cast into the lions' den. Now, O king, establish the injunction and sign the document so that it may not be changed, according to the law of the Medes and Persians, which may not be revoked." Therefore King Darius signed the document, that is, the injunction.*
>
> *Now when Daniel knew that the document was signed, he*

entered his house (now in his roof chamber he had windows open toward Jerusalem); and he continued kneeling on his knees three times a day, praying and giving thanks before his God, as he had been doing previously. Then these men came by agreement and found Daniel making petition and supplication before his God. Then they approached and spoke before the king about the king's injunction. "Did you not sign an injunction that any man who makes a petition to any god or man besides you, O king, for thirty days, is to be cast into the lions' den?" The king answered and said, "The statement is true, according to the law of the Medes and Persians, which may not be revoked." Then they answered and spoke before the king. "Daniel, who is one of the exiles from Judah, pays no attention to you, O king, or to the injunction which you signed, but keeps making his petition three times a day." Then, as soon as the king heard this statement, he was deeply distressed and set his mind on delivering Daniel; and even until sunset he kept exerting himself to rescue him. Then these men came by agreement to the king and said to the king, "Recognize, O king, that it is a law of the Medes and Persians that no injunction or statute which the king establishes may be changed."

Then the king gave orders, and Daniel was brought in and cast into the lions' den (vv. 5–16).

Thankfully, justice won out. God safely delivered Daniel from the lions, and King Darius tossed the deceivers into the den in his place . . . and they were history.

ABIDING PRINCIPLES WE NEED TO REMEMBER

With what I have written thus far as a basis, I want to dig deeper into how all of it applies today. In the process, I want to leave with you three principles I hope you will never forget.

These principles are neither popular nor easy to apply, but I believe them with my whole heart. Furthermore, I commit myself to abide by them, regardless of the reaction they may cause. I plead with you: Before you turn me off or sit down to write me a rebuttal, think. Think clearly. Most of all, think biblically. Ask yourself why you feel so defensive. Go to the Scriptures (as I have done and will continue to do) to support your position. You may be surprised to discover your disagreement with me sounds plausible and logical, but lacks *biblical* justification.

First: *True integrity implies you do what is right when no one is looking or when everyone is compromising.*

You may have to admit that you have several things needing your immediate attention. Don't delay . . . start today. Your integrity demands it. It is never too late to start doing what is right. Clean up your act or be man or woman enough to admit your hypocrisy—especially if you are in ministry.

Ministry is a character profession. To put it bluntly, you can sleep around and still be a good brain surgeon. You can cheat on your mate and have little trouble continuing to practice law. Apparently, it is no problem to stay in politics and plagiarize. You can be a successful salesperson and cheat on your income tax. But you cannot do those things as a Christian or as a minister and continue enjoying the Lord's blessing. You must do right in order to have true integrity. If you can't come to terms with evil or break habits that continue to bring reproach to the name of Christ, please, do the Lord (and us in ministry) a favor and resign.

I am not alone in these strong convictions. There are others who have become weary of the integrity crisis of our times and have addressed it in a bold manner.

> Where can people turn for truth? Philosophers remember old Diogenes, who still symbolizes the search because he went around truth-seeking with a lantern in broad daylight. . . .
>
> Some religious leaders do serve as models. . . . The hard times this year were for the religious prime-time characters. Some TV evangelists were unfaithful to their spouses and others doctored their autobiographies to cover past dissembling. The cynical public overlooks the model min-

istry down the block and says to the celebrities, "Get your own act together and we might pay attention again. . . ."

. . . the public search for truth is based on definitions that differ somewhat from most concepts of classic and modern philosophy. There is a modern clue for the present search from the language of the religion that dominates in the West, one based on biblical meanings. The ancient Hebrews and the authors of the Greek New Testament spoke little about truth in the abstract, about truth in the impersonal sense. Instead they connected "truth" with the character of a faithful God and then wanted to see that quality reflected in humans.

The biblical concept richer than "telling the truth" is expressed as "doing the truth." When someone "does" the truth, we can check that person out more readily than when talk about truth is only an intellectual game or tease.

"Doing the truth" relied on the Hebrew concept of *emeth*, connoting faithfulness and reliability. . . . The truth is "in" them and they "are" truth because they "do" truth: We say they have integrity.

The test of such truth is obvious. Say, "she's as good as her word" or "his handshake is better than a contract!" and you describe someone who embodies what today's truth seekers are looking for. . . .

The liars and deceivers of recent exposure were so often loners, celebrities who had admirers and groupies but not friends who could be critical, who could keep them honest.

. . . Character requires context. The French novelist Stendhal wrote that "One can acquire anything in solitude except character." . . .[33]

Second: *Real integrity stays in place whether the test is adversity or prosperity.* If you really have integrity, a demotion or promotion won't change you. Your inner core won't be dislodged. But I should repeat my earlier warning: Others won't like it if you don't "go along" with the system. Be ready for misunderstanding from the mediocre crowd. You will surely encounter their hostility.

I received a letter from a young woman that describes how intense the pressure to maintain integrity can become. I will include only a segment of what she wrote:

> . . . I hold an undergraduate degree in microbiology and a graduate degree in medical librarianship. In my early thirties it became clear to me that I would prefer a career in medicine, so I enrolled in a one-year premed program at a local college . . . to do the course work, prepare for the standardized exams and apply to medical schools. I was not on campus very long before I became aware of a pervasive demoralization among faculty and staff: the kind of thing which can only be due to very bad management.
>
> It was also abundantly plain that my classmates were extremely dishonest: falsifying laboratory records, cheating on tests, and pressuring me to do likewise, etc. The pressure was no problem; I know how to resist pressure. But the professor in charge of the program is a man struggling with the twin demons of a mid-life crisis and a deplorable working environment. Under this intense pressure, his favorite phrase has become, "I don't want to know!" I could not bring myself to add to his burdens. Given a choice between intellectual integrity and compassion, I chose compassion. Bad choice. Obviously foolish. I was wrong. Out of my depth. In the end, I had no choice but to force him to face what he had to know.
>
> Things muddled along until March when some . . . were caught cheating on a take-home exam we had been instructed to work on independently. The culprits—I was not among them—defended themselves on the basis that they did not know that they were doing anything wrong. As part of the criteria for admission we were expected to agree to support each other under any and all conditions.

This is supposed to ensure against cut-throat competition, but it backfired. The professor went before the disciplinary board and endorsed the students' behavior, thereby compromising his own integrity and that of the institution.

At that point, I felt strongly that I had been silent too long. Too late, I protested (as gently as I could—no point in hitting the nerve with a sledgehammer) on the grounds that attempting to force the medical schools to accept fifteen highly unscrupulous people has devastating implications for society, as well as for the people who do such things. I cannot consider this a trivial incident. Dishonest students become dishonest professionals. When chemistry-based professionals are dishonest, people die! There's nothing trivial about that.

My words fell on deaf ears. Throughout this time my academic performance had been inferior; I do not perform well under such conditions . . . so I was told that I am hopelessly incompetent and not worth knowing. To which I retorted that I have character and that's more important than grades. Or medical school. Or money. . . .[34]

Real integrity stays in place whether you pass or fail. I admire that lady. She doesn't claim to be perfect, but she does desire to be a woman of strong character.

My third principle will be the most controversial: *Broken moral integrity means the spiritual leader forfeits the right to lead.*

Before you wrestle with me on this, pause and think. I would encourage you to support your position from the Bible, not your feelings or the opinions of others. While you're at it, I would challenge you to find in the Scriptures people who once occupied places of high-visibility leadership in ministry who, after moral failure, were later placed back on the same pinnacle and experienced the same or greater success in their ministry. I have searched for years and have not found ONE biblical example. There is not a single person who fits that model in the New Testament.

In the Old Testament, David is the only one who comes close. But if you do a careful study of that man's life, you will see that his leadership looks like a housetop. He goes up, up, up . . . until Bathsheba. Prior to the adulterous affair, David was at the zenith of his career. Afterwards, everything goes down, down, down. Defeat on the battlefield. Trouble at home. His son rapes a half-sister, Tamar. Another son leads a rebellion against him. David ultimately dies heartbroken, his family in disarray and his successor (Solomon) primed for an even greater fall. He was allowed to remain a king (not a spiritual office, by the way), but his authority and the public's respect were never as great. I suggest that not even David qualifies as a model of a fallen leader who returned to the full blessing of God and the respect of the people. It has been my observation that such examples simply cannot be found in the Word of God.

Some of you reading these words will assume I lack a forgiving spirit. That is simply not the truth. I can and will continue to forgive the grossest sin, but in this case, forgiveness is not the issue; the *broken integrity* of a minister is. I have no problem forgiving any brother or sister who breaks his or her moral integrity. I have great trouble, however, reappointing that individual back in the same high-level place of authority.

Why? Two reasons: First, because I do not find biblical justification for or examples of that occurring; second, because certain failures reveal deep-seated character flaws (not merely sinfulness) that created distrust among those being led. If you are thinking that Jonah or Peter qualify as models, remember that neither of them fell morally. Theirs was not a sexual failure. I consider that a category unto itself, and I do so with biblical justification. For some reason very few Christians have either studied or taken seriously the following Scripture:

> The one who commits adultery with a woman is lacking sense; he who would destroy himself does it. Wounds and disgrace he will find, and his reproach will not be blotted out (Proverbs 6:32–33).

I would call that clear and direct, yet it seems as though ministers who have compromised sexually no longer hesitate to return to their positions of public responsibilities in spite of the statement that such "reproach will not be blotted out." This cannot help but puzzle many in the pew who have difficulty seeing beyond the minister's wounds, disgrace, and his unerasable reproach.

Some time ago a friend of mine was troubled over the number of ministers who were falling into sexual sins, only to be placed back in similar leadership roles within a period of time. Something didn't seem right about that to my friend so he asked me how I viewed the issue. I thought long and hard before I wrote back. Please read the following excerpts from my letter very carefully.

Like it or not, accept it or not, we cannot ignore that Scripture does draw a distinction between the common, everyday, all-too-familiar sins in life and the deliberate acting out of sexual sins. This would especially include sexual sins that express themselves in lengthy deception and secret escapades which culminate in scandalous affairs that disrupt entire families, corrupting (and usually destroying) once solid marriages. Often, hidden immorality goes on for months—even years—while the one practicing such deeds in private lives a complete lie in public.

The sheer shamelessness, insanity, and audacity of it all reveals deep-seated character flaws. Those flaws cause the immoral person involved in the perversion to sin "against his own body" and thus enter into a unique category of disobedience unlike "every other sin." My observations are based on 1 Corinthians 6:18, which deserves careful study:

"Flee immorality. Every other sin that a man commits is outside the body, but the immoral man sins against his own body."

Am I suggesting that such shameless and deplorable actions cannot be forgiven? Of course not. But I am admitting that the character flaws which led to those extended and deceptive acts of sensuality may very well restrict such individuals from places of public service they once knew and enjoyed. . . . By their sinning "against their own body," they reveal a weakness in their moral character, which sets in motion certain consequences and many complications. All this can scandalize the body of Christ if they are brought back before the public to enjoy all the privileges and rights that once were theirs. It asks too much of those who were deceived and offended to expect them to say "I forgive," then quietly step aside as the newly forgiven brother or sister moves back into a high-visibility ministry before the general public. . . .

We have an interesting analogy in our system of jurisprudence. A person guilty of a felony may serve time behind bars, become a model prisoner, acknowledge his or her wrong actions, and finally be freed, pardoned from the crime of the past. But he or she forfeits the right to vote for the rest of his or her life. Fair or not, appropriate or not, that special privilege of participating in our nation's future he or she once enjoyed is forever removed. . . .

Being granted the privilege of public leadership and ministry carries with it the tenuous yet essential presence of power. In Christian service, that power is incredibly influential and can be used for selfish purposes, all the while appearing gracious. The temptation to deceive is especially strong in handling such power. Thus the constant need for accountability, self-restraint, and strong discipline. One whose life has been marked by a gross lack of such traits reveals his or her weakness of character in this area, thus damaging others' trust and confidence.

It's not a matter of forgiveness, I repeat, but of forfeiting certain rights and privileges. Though God fully forgave, you recall, He kept Moses from the Promised Land, demoted Saul from ruling as king, and restrained David from building the temple. Each may have been forgiven, yet each was nevertheless divinely restricted from the fulfillment of his dreams.

Is repentance then without value? On the contrary, without repentance the vertical relationship with God remains hindered, and the horizontal relationship with others remains crippled. Furthermore, confession and repentance allow the forgiven to glean God's wisdom from His reproofs and to reestablish a measure of restored harmony with those who were offended in the backwash of that person's sins. Repentance not only validates the sinner's confession, it prompts the offended to fully forgive. . . .

I must add one more thought. There is too little said these days about the value of a broken and contrite heart. The forgiven sinner of today is often one who expects (dare I say *demands?*) more than he or she should. Scripture calls this "presumption." A broken and contrite heart is not presumptuous; it makes no demands, entertains no expectations. I've noticed that those recovering from a sexual scandal sometimes judge rather harshly others who are reluctant to allow them all the leadership they once exercised. I've often heard them refer to this as "shooting our wounded" when, in fact, those most wounded are the people who trusted when the fallen leader was living a lie.

My question is: Who's shooting whom? A presumptuous spirit usually reveals itself in an aggressive desire to return to a platform of public ministry. When that desire isn't granted, those being restrained can easily present themselves as pathetic, helpless victims of other's judgment and condemnation. I find that response manipulative and quite disturbing. . . .

What concerns me most about this whole scenario is an absence of abject submission to God and utter humility before others. I am occasionally stunned by the unrealistic expectations of those who have left numerous people in their wake. Some even point fingers of accusation at those in the body who resist their returning to public ministry. Many are still trying to believe that their once-trusted friend, mate, relative, or hero could have fallen so far and lived such a lie. The truly repentant soul, it seems to me, should be so overwhelmed by humiliation and so grateful for the grace of God, he or she has no room for fawning pride within or frowning accusation without. David, after the Bathsheba affair simply prayed, "Restore to me the joy of Thy salvation, and sustain me with a willing spirit" (Psalm 51:12). To him that was sufficient.[35]

As I said earlier, ministry is a character profession. God's divine calling places it into a distinct category with a stricter standard than all others. If you question that, read 1 Timothy 3:1–7 and try to imagine its applying to any other calling than the ministry. Even Charles Haddon Spurgeon—a man of enormous grace—held strict convictions on this subject.

> I hold very stern opinions with regard to Christian men who have fallen into gross sin; I rejoice that they may be truly converted, and may be with mingled hope and caution received into the church; but I question, gravely question whether a man who has grossly sinned should be very readily restored to the pulpit.[36]

A SOLEMN SERIES OF WARNINGS

In light of our need for ministers with unbroken integrity, I think it might help us to ponder a few pointed warnings. Rather than make up a list of my own, I would rather quote A. W. Tozer, who, being dead, still speaks.

> The ministry is one of the most perilous of professions. . . .
> Satan knows that the downfall of a prophet of God is a strategic victory for him, so he rests not day or night devising hidden snares and dead-falls for the ministry. Perhaps a better figure would be the poison dart that only

paralyzes its victim, for I think that Satan has little interest in killing the preacher outright. An ineffective, half-alive minister is a better advertisement for hell than a good man dead. So the preacher's dangers are likely to be spiritual rather than physical. . . .

There are indeed some very real dangers of the grosser sort which the minister must guard against, such as love of money and women; but the deadliest perils are far more subtle than these. . . .

There is, for one, the danger that the minister shall come to think of himself as belonging to a privileged class. Our "Christian" society tends to increase this danger by granting the clergy discounts and other courtesies, and the church itself helps a bad job along by bestowing upon men of God various sonorous honorifics which are either comical or awe-inspiring, depending upon how you look at them. . . .

Another danger is that he may develop a perfunctory spirit in the performance of the work of the Lord. Familiarity may breed contempt even at the altar of God. How frightful a thing it is for the preacher when he becomes accustomed to his work, when his sense of wonder departs, when he gets used to the unusual, when he loses his solemn fear in the presence of the High and Holy One; when, to put it bluntly, he gets a little bored with God and heavenly things.

If anyone should doubt that this can happen let him read the Old Testament and see how the priests of Jehovah sometimes lost their sense of divine mystery and became profane even as they performed their holy duties. And church history reveals that this tendency toward perfunctoriness did not die with the passing of the Old Testament order. Secular priests and pastors who keep the doors of God's house for bread are still among us.

Satan will see to it that they are, for they do the cause of God more injury than a whole army of atheists would do.

There is the danger also that the preacher may suffer alienation of spirit from the plain people. This arises from the nature of institutionalized Christianity. The minister meets religious people almost exclusively. People are on their guard when they are with him. They tend to talk over their own heads and to be for the time the kind of persons they think he wants them to be rather than the kind of persons they are in fact. This creates a world of unreality where no one is quite himself, but the preacher has lived in it so long that he accepts it as real and never knows the difference.

The results of living in this artificial world are disastrous. . . .

Another peril that confronts the minister is that he may come unconsciously to love religious and philosophic ideas rather than saints and sinners. It is altogether possible to feel for the world of lost men the same kind of detached affection that the naturalist Fabre, say, felt for a hive of bees or a hill of black ants. They are something to study, to learn from, possibly even to help, but nothing to weep over or die for. . . .

Another trap into which the preacher is in danger of falling is that he may do what comes naturally and just take it easy. I know how ticklish this matter is and, while my writing this will not win me friends, I hope it may influence people in the right direction. It is easy for the minister to be turned into a privileged idler, a social parasite with an open palm and an expectant look. He has no boss within sight; he is not often required to keep regular hours, so he can work out a comfortable pattern of life that permits him to loaf, putter, play, doze and run about at his pleasure. And many do just that.

To avoid this danger the minister should voluntarily work hard.[37]

THE ESSENTIAL VALUE OF ACCOUNTABILITY

Tozer's words penetrate. But we need more than warnings. Counsel that admonishes us to behave ourselves can only go so far in helping us "buffet" our bodies and guard us against disqualification (1 Corinthians 9:27). To make the one-two punch more effective, personal accountability is invaluable. Since I have already addressed this subject in two previous books,[38] there is no reason for me to repeat myself in great detail here. But allow me to underscore, once again, how *essential* accountability is to maintaining a pure life before others and a wholesome walk with God.

Self-analysis is healthy and good. Time alone before the Lord must remain top priority. But we cannot stop there. Being creatures with blind spots and tendencies toward rationalization, we must also be in close touch with a few trustworthy individuals with whom we meet on a regular basis. Knowing that such an encounter is going to happen helps us hold the line morally and ethically. I know of nothing more effective for maintaining a pure heart and keeping one's life balanced and on target than being a part of an accountability group. It is amazing what such a group can provide to help us hold our passions in check!

Recently, I was encouraged to hear about a minister who meets once a week with a small group of men. They are committed to one another's purity. They pray with and for each other. They talk openly and honestly about their struggles, weaknesses, temptations, and trials. In addition to these general things, they look one another in the eye as they ask and answer no less than seven specific questions:

1. Have you been with a woman this week in such a way that was inappropriate or could have looked to others that you were using poor judgment?

2. Have you been completely above reproach in all your financial dealings this week?

3. Have you exposed yourself to any explicit material this week?

4. Have you spent time daily in prayer and in the Scriptures this week?

5. Have you fulfilled the mandate of your calling this week?

6. Have you taken time off to be with your family this week?

7. Have you just lied to me?

I would call that being accountable! Yes, such meetings can be exacting and even painful. But if it can help curb carnality and keep the minister's life free from secrets that will some day result in scandal, I'm convinced it is worth it. I challenge all of us to risk being that vulnerable on a regular basis.

It's time for the church to remember the value of integrity in our relationship with Christ and in our walk with Him upon this earth. That means recommiting ourselves to a ministry anointed with power and godly purity. Let's make a firm statement to ministers in training at seminaries across the land. Let's remind them that they are being entrusted with a high and holy privilege, which, if perverted, will result in their forfeiting the right to lead God's people. I am convinced if they know that going in, more will walk in the fear of God after graduation. By His grace, they will finish well. Let's put dignity back where it belongs: in the church of Jesus Christ. Let's cause people to sit up and notice our kind of ministry is worth their time, their trust, and their treasure.

No one ever said it better than Josiah Holland:

> GOD, GIVE US MEN! *A time like this demands*
> *Strong minds, great hearts, true faith and ready hands;*
> *Men whom the lust of office does not kill;*
> *Men whom the spoils of office cannot buy;*
> *Men who possess opinions and a will;*
> *Men who have honor; men who will not lie;*
> *Men who can stand before a demagogue*
> *And damn his treacherous flatteries without winking!*
> *Tall men, sun-crowned, who live above the fog*
> *In public duty and in private thinking;*

For while the rabble, with their thumb-worn creeds,
Their large professions and their little deeds,
Mingle in selfish strife, lo! Freedom weeps,
Wrong rules the land and waiting Justice sleeps.[39]

As we shall see in the final chapter, it is time to restore respect for the ministry.

1. What promises or commitments have you made in the past two weeks? (This would include the times you have said, "I'll be praying with you about that" or, "I'll take care of that right away.") List them, and by God's enabling, *do what you said you would do*.

2. Do you have a friend or friends—preferably of the same sex—who hold you accountable on a regular basis? It's easy to mentally agree with the concept of accountability, but it takes determination (dare I say "guts"?) to follow through and *do* something about it. I challenge you to take the first step TODAY by writing down the names of Christian friends who might be willing to meet with you regularly on a long-term basis for this very purpose. Let me strongly encourage you, in light of the "savage" times in which we live, to contact one or more of those individuals this week.

3. Go back to the "Hall of Faith" in Hebrews 11. Read the chapter through several times, running your hand over the keen edges of these exemplary lives. Ask the Lord to lift your vision and kindle your faith as you meditate on these words.

RESTORING RESPECT FOR THE MINISTRY

I have a friend I have known and loved for thirty years. During that period of time we have been inseparable. Our friendship has deepened as my appreciation for this friend has intensified.

In recent years my friend has come upon hard times. We have continued to get along beautifully, but others have begun to misunderstand and malign. It has hurt me to hear all the ugly things being said. Even though my friend has done nothing wrong and has taken the brunt of unfair, exaggerated, and sarcastic remarks—not to mention all the unfounded and caustic accusations—there seems to be no letup. It has gotten so bad on occasions I've wondered if there can be a full recovery. In spite of all that has been said against my dear friend, our commitment has remained firm and true for thirty-five years.

My friend is the ministry.

I was called to the ministry while in the Marines, sometime between 1957 and 1959. That was when I first realized God's hand was unquestionably on my life. This realization changed the direction of my future from a familiar career I had assumed I should pursue to an unfamiliar calling I had never before considered even a remote possibility. Slowly and deliberately, God made it clear that I should return to school, get a solid theological education at a respected seminary, and spend the balance of my life in the gospel ministry.

The friendship had begun.

Refusing to fight the call of God any longer, I enrolled in Dallas Theological Seminary late in the spring of 1959. Cynthia and I subsequently moved to a tiny campus apartment that summer, and before I knew it I was neck deep in theology, church history, Greek, Hebrew, Christian education, missions, hermeneutics, homiletics, apologetics—the whole nine yards. What a challenge! She and I absolutely loved it. The studies were stretching but incredibly rewarding.

The friendship with the ministry which had begun earlier was now deepening. Little did I realize how fulfilling it would be. With the exception of my marriage and the delights of home and family, to this day nothing comes close to the joys connected with this growing friendship. Not once have I looked back and regretted it. In spite of the tough days, I cannot imagine any friendship more satisfying.

I graduated in 1963, and shortly thereafter was officially ordained into the ministry. We did not have the foggiest idea where or how God would ultimately use us. All we knew was that we loved each other, we loved Him, and we were prepared, available, and ready to serve.

I smile when I think back on those simple and innocent days in the early 1960s. How little we knew, and yet how committed we were to this lifetime friendship with something we held in highest esteem—the ministry.

Numerous changes have transpired over these thirty-five years. Back then the ministry was greatly respected. Ministers who moved their families into a community were welcomed and respected. They were considered an asset, people of dignity, deserving of the community's unqualified trust. The role and responsibilities of a pastor were unquestionably esteemed. There was no suspicion, no reservation, only high regard for the man who stood in the pulpit and proclaimed God's message. In those days "a man of God" was still the descriptive title of the local minister who led a flock, rejoiced with them in their celebrations, comforted them in their grief, and lived an exemplary life before them.

Understand, this was not because all ministers were considered superhuman models of perfection. None of us walked on water. Many then, as now, entered this calling out of backgrounds that were anything but pristine. The apostle Paul is a case in point. His testimony never hid the fact that he did not deserve his calling into ministry:

> *I thank Christ Jesus our Lord, who has strengthened me, because He considered me faithful, putting me into service; even though I was formerly a blasphemer and a persecutor and a violent aggressor. And yet I was shown mercy, because I acted ignorantly in unbelief; and the grace of our Lord was more than abundant, with the faith and love which are found in Christ Jesus. It is a trustworthy statement, deserving full acceptance, that Christ Jesus came into the world to save sinners, among whom I am foremost of all. And yet for this reason I found mercy, in order that in me as the foremost, Jesus Christ might demonstrate His perfect patience, as an example for those who would believe in Him for eternal life (1 Timothy 1:12–16).*

Don't miss "I was formerly a blasphemer . . . persecutor . . . violent aggressor . . . yet I was shown mercy . . . grace was more than abundant." There isn't a minister alive today—nor has there ever been—who couldn't write similar words.

My point is this: Back then, in spite of a minister's humanity, quirks, and imperfections, his office and his authority were respected. No longer! Today, even though ministry standards remain the highest of any calling or profession, even though the minister's role still rests upon pillars of purity, integrity, humility, discipline, commitment, and trust, public opinion of the ministry has never been lower. Certainly, it has never been lower in the history of America.

I am not suggesting there has never been criticism (some justified) against those in ministry. In every generation there have been a few who brought shame to their calling. In addition, there have always been controversial ministers and a host of unusual characters—maverick types—in the ranks of the clergy. Many have been misunderstood and others simply disagreed with, which is certainly understandable. But when the facts were in, when close scrutiny yielded the unvarnished truth, few were proven to be deceivers and downright hypocritical. The ministry as a whole was not hurt by those individuals. That can no longer be said. In this generation especially, the ministry is now viewed with the same jaded suspicion as other once respected positions of responsibility. I could not agree more with the man who wrote:

> I've come to the conclusion that the one word that best describes the evangelical church situation today is *reproach*, and I have a feeling that many people agree with me. In fact, *reproach* is the one word that seems to describe other areas of society besides the church: the sports arena, the embassy, the halls of academe, the White House, the Pentagon, Wall Street, Capitol Hill, and even the day-care center. Scandal seems to be the order of our day. . . . No wonder *Time* asked in [a recent] cover story . . . "What Ever Happened To Ethics?". . .
>
> Our problem is not that the public has suddenly found sinners in the church, much to the embarrassment of Christians. No, the public has known about sin in the church for a long time; and somehow the church has survived. Evangelical Christians today are not like a group of schoolchildren, standing around blushing because we were caught breaking the rules. We are more like a defeated army, naked before our enemies, and unable to fight back because they have made a frightening discovery: the church is lacking in integrity. . . .

For nineteen centuries, the church has been telling the world to admit its sins, repent, and believe the gospel. Today, in the twilight of the twentieth century, the world is telling the church to face up to her sins, repent, and *start being the true church of that gospel*. We Christians boast that we are not ashamed of the gospel of Christ, but perhaps the gospel of Christ is ashamed of us. For some reason, our ministry doesn't match our message. . . .[40]

REALISTIC GLIMPSES OF THE SHAMEFUL SCENE

I realize that few people need to read through a detailed litany of ministry ills that have led to the mess we're in. But perhaps a few realistic glimpses will help us see why the public now sneers instead of cheers. To conserve time and space, I will list some of the more notorious examples.

- In the late 1960s, the ministry became a reason for dodging the draft. You want to stay out of Vietnam? Easy: Claim you are called to the ministry!

- In the 1970s, religious cults reached national prominence. Weird gurus led innocent/ignorant idealists astray. Some occupied land in Oregon, others moved en masse to another country . . . leading to a mass suicide in "Jonestown" where over nine hundred drank poison.

- Divorce and adultery invaded the church as sheep and shepherd alike showed little concern. More and more ministers bought into the system, creating an epidemic-like atmosphere in the church. Rationalization reigned supreme.

- The 1980s ushered in a new era: the "electronic church." What was once limited to a few local churches was now being televised for all to see, the good as well as the bad. Especially the bad. All it took was a preacher who could draw a crowd and raise enough money to buy the time. Less emphasis on character, more on charisma.

- One televangelist went up into a so-called "prayer tower" and promised never to return unless several million dollars were contributed. The press had a field day.

- The PTL scandal followed shortly thereafter, which led to an exposé of such disgraceful events even the secular world was shocked. Everything from talk shows to T-shirts capitalized on the smear for months.

- The following year another televangelist confessed to being involved in sexual deviations, which *Penthouse* magazine exploited by interviewing the alleged prostitute and having her describe in detail what she did . . . with lurid photographs attached. The man said he would accept the discipline his denomination felt appropriate, but later ignored their counsel, resigned from that realm of accountability, and is still on the tube.

- I shall restrain from including the ever-increasing list of names of evangelical pastors, authors, missionaries, Christian leaders, musicians, singers, educators, counselors, youth workers, high-profile laymen and women in the church, who have compromised their testimony and broken the public's trust through adultery, homosexuality, substance abuse, financial irresponsibility, personal unaccountability, legal battles, and even criminal activity. And, remember, these have been people *in ministry*.

I ask you, if you were a non-Christian, wouldn't you have less respect for the ministry today? The fallout has been dreadful. Even ministries of integrity are now being viewed with suspicion. Brother-bashing and sister-smashing is now "in." Everybody is fair game. Perhaps the saddest dimension of all are the innocent lives close to those who have fallen and failed so scandalously. I'm thinking of whole church congregations who must go on after discovering that their minister lived deceitfully in immorality. Think also of the faculty members and students who are left in the wake of a president or some campus leader who brought reproach to the name of Christ. And how about the mate and children who have to pick up the pieces because of their husband's and father's careless and selfish indulgence? And don't forget fellow church-staff personnel whose future is uncertain because their leader lived a lie.

What grieves me most is that my long-time, faithful-and-true friend has been brutally victimized. The ministry has been dragged into a sleazy back alley, kicked, punched, assaulted, raped, and robbed of respect. The bruises and scars can no longer be ignored. Face it, even though the great majority in ministry continue to defend and uphold the highest standards, the ministry itself has been severely crippled. Christian-crushing has become the media's favorite indoor sport.

This is not meant to sound like Elijah's lament, "I, alone, am left." I am fully aware that pride has no place in any of our lives. Those who think they stand must continually take heed lest they fall. No one is immune to temptation. All of us are capable of falling. (I remind myself of that fact *every week* of my life.) Nevertheless, I believe it is time to awaken the church to the need to restore respect for the ministry. Long enough have we sat back, licked our wounds, sighed about how many are falling, and passively shrugged our shoulders, lamenting that "we must be living in the last days." Of course we are! But does that mean we should do nothing more than fold our arms and grimly take our lumps? In no way!

Few are more burdened for purity in ministry than a man all of us have grown to admire, former presidential assistant Chuck

Colson. God has used him to stir up the church of Jesus Christ in these days of compromise. While he was on an interview tour speaking about his book *Kingdoms in Conflict,* he observed much that troubled him, especially the Christian-bashing attitude of the secular media. He describes it vividly:

> The red "on the air" light flashed, and the seventy-fifth interview of my *Kingdoms in Conflict* tour was underway. It felt like the seven hundred-fiftieth; for weeks I had been in and out of commercial television and radio stations across America, talking about church, state, and Christianity's role in public life.
>
> At least I was getting a broad exposure to secular attitude. It's good to leave our evangelical cocoons periodically and find out what people really think of us. But what I found was sobering—to say the least.
>
> This day's session was typical. "Today we're interviewing Charles Colson," my host said smoothly. "But first, let's hear from 'God's little goofballs.'" With that he flipped a switch, and a prerecorded message from Jim and Tammy Bakker filled the studio. I'm not sure, but I think the inspirational recording included Tammy's recipe for three-layer bean dip. The interviewer grinned. "And now, we have another evangelist with us today. Let's hear what Chuck Colson has to say."
>
> The majority of my nearly 100 interviews began in a similar manner. Christian-bashing is very much in fashion these days. The Bakker affair has produced a comic caricature of all Christians and derision that runs deeper than most of us realize.
>
> At first I was defensive. But as the interviews continued I got angry. What about the 350,000 churches across America where people's needs are quietly being met? I asked. The thousands of missionaries to the poor, the army of Christian volunteers who faithfully go into prisons each week? Why does the media focus instead on the flamboy-

ant few? It's not fair, I argued, to stereotype the whole church; we're not all hypocrites out to pad our own pockets.

But my interviewer simply smiled. Reason, after all, is no match for ridicule.[41]

Yet that is not the way Christ looks at His Bride. And we can still turn heads around. My plea, as I stated earlier, is that we finish well. In doing so we can begin to restore much of the respect we have lost over the last three decades. I challenge each one of us to start today.

HELPFUL FACTS THAT ARE EASILY FORGOTTEN

Let's return to a familiar scriptural commentary on our times. Though we have looked at it before, a second glance is necessary.

But the Spirit explicitly says that in later times some will fall away from the faith, paying attention to deceitful spirits and doctrines of demons, by means of the hypocrisy of liars seared in their own conscience as with a branding iron, men who forbid marriage and advocate abstaining from foods, which God has created to be gratefully shared in by those who believe and know the truth. For everything created by God is good, and nothing is to be rejected, if it is received with gratitude; for it is sanctified by means of the word of God and prayer.

In pointing out these things to the brethren, you will be a good servant of Christ Jesus, constantly nourished on the words of the faith and of the sound doctrine which you have been following (1 Timothy 4:1–6).

If I understand those last words correctly, it is the responsibility of a good minister to point out to others that last days mean hard times. I have been communicating that for several chapters. While certain things should alarm us, absolutely nothing should overwhelm us. "The Spirit explicitly says" we can expect the worst. When it occurs we know we have entered God's final plans for this old globe. It's getting close to quittin' time!

Since that is true, it is easy to focus on only the obvious—the overt wickedness—and forget a few facts that will counteract feeling overwhelmed. Three come to my mind.

First, *Scripture predicts and warns us of such times*. If we have learned nothing else in my previous chapters, we have learned that such things as those I just listed will not only happen, they will also get worse. That is why the term *epidemic* is appropriate. I doubt that anyone in Spurgeon's day or Moody's generation would have described the divorce problem in the church or the sexual promiscuity among Christians as being "epidemic." But that describes *our* day, without a doubt. There were people in the ministry who fell in their day, but the numbers were nothing like they are today. Furthermore, the scandals were not as prevalent *in the church* as they are today. Clearly, as Scripture predicts, wrong is on the rise, and it will crescendo to a greater degree the closer we get to Christ's return.

I could list twelve to fifteen compelling references in Scripture, but only a couple will suffice, one from Jesus' teachings, another from Jude, as he quotes Jesus:

> *And Jesus answered and said to them, "See to it that no one misleads you. For many will come in My name, saying, 'I am the Christ,' and will mislead many. And you will be hearing of wars and rumors of wars; see that you are not frightened, for those things must take place, but that is not yet the end. . . .*
>
> *"And at that time many will fall away and will deliver up one another and hate one another. And many false prophets will arise, and will mislead many. And because lawlessness is increased, most people's love will grow cold. . . .*
>
> *"Then, if any one says to you, 'Behold, here is the Christ,' or 'There He is,' do not believe him. For false Christs and false prophets will arise and will show great signs and wonders, so as to mislead, if possible, even the elect. Behold, I have told you in advance"* (Matthew 24:4–6, 10–12, 23–25).
>
> *But you, beloved, ought to remember the words that were spoken beforehand by the apostles of our Lord Jesus Christ, that*

they were saying to you, "In the last time there shall be mock-
ers, following after their own ungodly lusts." These are the ones
who cause divisions, worldly-minded, devoid of the Spirit. But
you, beloved, building yourselves up on your most holy faith;
praying in the Holy Spirit; keep yourselves in the love of God,
waiting anxiously for the mercy of our Lord Jesus Christ to eter-
nal life. And have mercy on some, who are doubting; save oth-
ers, snatching them out of the fire; and on some have mercy
with fear, hating even the garment polluted by the flesh (Jude
17–23).

Second, *the actual percentage of those in ministry who fall is quite
small.* It will help if you and I remind ourselves that for every one
whose moral failure makes the news, there are thousands upon
thousands more who remain faithful, diligent, pure messengers of
Christ. The vast majority of those who promised years ago to serve
the Lord and model His truth are still doing so today. A realistic
perspective will keep us balanced in our thinking and optimistic
in our outlook. When we start to believe we are all alone in the
battle, the adversary does a number on us.

I call that kind of thinking "the Elijah syndrome." Remember
when the prophet slumped into a depression, fled into the woods,
and prayed for the Lord to take his life? The story recorded in 1
Kings 19 is worth your time. Not only did he run because he was
intimidated by the dominating witch Jezebel who ruled Ahab's
throne, he ran because he thought he was on a solo mission in
ministry. He really believed there was no one else quite as dedicated as he. That really gets to you! Look at Elijah's "testimony"
as he licked his wounds:

*I have been very zealous for the LORD, the God of hosts; for the
sons of Israel have forsaken Thy covenant, torn down Thine
altars and killed Thy prophets with the sword. And I alone am
left; and they seek my life, to take it away* (v. 14).

Without hesitation God interrupted his pity party and informed
him there were seven thousand others, like Elijah, who had not

bowed to Baal. It did something to the lonely, burnt-out prophet when he realized the percentage of the faithless in ministry was really quite slight. It will help us to keep that in mind as a few of our heroes in ministry fail and fall. A few may be guilty of gross sins, but most have not come close to bowing the knee to Baal. Remember that as you continue pressing on.

Third, *human imperfection includes ministers*. I have mentioned this earlier, but it seems significant enough to be repeated and amplified.

When God calls individuals into His vineyard, He calls only sinful people. Not even one could claim perfection. Each is inadequate in himself, weak and wayward by nature, and could pose for a portrait painted in the lyrics of the beloved hymn "prone to wander . . . prone to leave the God I love."[42]

Do you question that? A quick review of biblical characters will help. Peter, the spokesman for the Twelve, openly and unhesitatingly denied his Lord only hours after promising he would be true though all the others walked away. John Mark deserted Paul and Barnabas on their first missionary journey at a crucial time when they needed all the help they could get. Demas, "having loved this present world," forsook Paul and fled to Thessalonica. Diotrephes, an early church leader, became a self-appointed "church boss."

The list would be incomplete if we limited it only to New Testament characters. Jonah, the pouting prophet, after he finally preached in Nineveh, evidenced prejudice, anger, and selfishness. Gehazi, Elisha's servant, couldn't hid his materialism and greed. David's adulterous affair, which led to murder and hypocrisy, is known to all. Isaiah admitted he was "a man of unclean lips." Aaron prompted the molding of a golden calf for the Hebrews to worship. Samson was a notorious womanizer.

And who can fully understand Solomon? If ever a man had a chance to bat 1.000 spiritually, Solomon did. Yet at the zenith of his career, when his fame and fortune were worldwide topics of discussion, when his influence was significant enough to impact vast kingdoms beyond his own, something snapped. Few have described Solomon's carnality better than G. Frederick Owen:

> Wisdom, loyalty, faithfulness, and efficiency characterized the attitudes and acts of David's brilliant son for the first few years of his reign. Then, as if he had attained the mastery of man and God, he turned from following the Lord, and selfishly seizing the reins of wrong, drove to the misty flats of licentiousness, pride and paganism.
>
> Maddened with the love of show, Solomon swung into a feverish career of wastefulness, impropriety, and oppression. Not satisfied with the necessary buildings and legitimate progress of his past years, he over-burdened his people with taxation, enslaved some, and ruthlessly instigated the murder of others. . . .
>
> His love for many women caused him to marry and pamper numerous foreign, heathen wives, who not only robbed him of his excellency of character, humility of spirit, and efficiency in state affairs, but dominated him and turned his heart to seek "after other gods. . . ."
>
> Solomon, like many another absolute monarch, drove too fast and traveled too far. . . . The monarch became debauched and effeminate; an egotist and cynic, so satiated with the sensual and material affairs of life that he became skeptical of all good—to him, all became "vanity and vexation of spirit."[43]

No one is immune to imperfection . . . none of the above and neither you nor I. If it can happen to them, it can happen to us. If you will remind yourself of these three things, it will help:

- Scripture warns us such things will occur.

- The percentage of those who fall is relatively small.

- Sinfulness and imperfection characterize everyone, including ministers.

UNALTERED STANDARD FOR THOSE IN MINISTRY

Does this mean we ought to lower the ministerial standard? In no way. Let everyone giving thought to entering vocational Christian service take note: The calling you are considering is high and holy. The requirements are exacting. The expectations almost unrealistic. I am of the opinion that not even the president of our country or the highest-paid person in the most responsible profession on earth is of greater significance than those called into the gospel ministry. Look before you leap. Think long and hard before you enroll in seminary. Be sure your mate is with you one hundred percent. If not, wait.

If you can be fulfilled in any other work, stay out of the ministry! Make an intense study of 1 Timothy 3:1–7; 4:12–16; 2 Timothy 4:1–5; Titus 1:5–9. Examine your motive. Pray. Think realistically. And while you are at it, spend a while thinking through James 3:1, which says:

Let not many of you become teachers, my brethren, knowing that as such we shall incur a stricter judgment.

To make that warning even clearer, notice how three others paraphrase the verse:

Don't aim at adding to the number of teachers, my brothers, I beg you! Remember that we who are teachers will be judged by a much higher standard (Phillips).

Dear brothers, don't be too eager to tell others their faults, for we all make many mistakes; and when we teachers of religion, who should know better, do wrong, our punishment will be greater than it would be for others (TLB).

. . . we teachers will be judged with special strictness (Moffatt).

It is time for us to realize who we are, fellow ministers. We, and those we lead, are the church, the Bride who stands beside Christ. He wants to "present to Himself the church in all her glory, having no spot or wrinkle or any such thing; but that she should be holy and blameless" (Ephesians 5:27). The bar—the standard—will never be lowered for ministry.

Young and older alike, most of the responsibility for restoring respect for the ministry rests with those of us who lead. This doesn't mean you are not free to be yourself. Nor does it mean you must never do the unusual or try out creative ideas or "break the mold" as a minister of the gospel. In my opinion, we need *more* fresh-thinking, unintimidated ministers who have the guts to model the true grace of God, not fearing what others may say or think.

But this does not suggest "sinning that grace may abound." We are called to carry out our tasks under the probing, pervasive, holy eye of God. No one faces a stricter analysis or a more exacting Judge than we. We need to fear man less and fear God more! Anyone entering seminary needs to accept that fact going in. My concern, quite honestly, is that some young men and women in seminary will think they are free to soften their moral standard because a few who have are back in ministry with no apparent damage.

While many of us are working hard to be ourselves and to combat legalism, let's be sure that we don't rationalize disobedience by calling it liberty. As James puts it, we will "be judged by a much higher standard."

WAYS TO AVOID DOUBT AND DEVASTATION

I want to close this chapter on a positive note by suggesting some practical ways to avoid being devastated by those in ministry who have fallen. Let me give you something to refuse, to remember, to release, and on which to refocus.

First, *refuse to deify anyone in the ministry.* Many folks make the mistake of allowing admiration to grow into exaltation. Bad choice! I don't care how gifted, how capable, or how much a minister has meant to you, if you exalt that person beyond proper bounds, *you* will fall further than anyone if *he* falls. Keep all ministers off the pedestal! Thrones are for kings and queens. Worship

is for the living God. Pedestals are for vases and flowers and sculptured busts of men and women now dead. Don't enthrone your
pastor—or any minister, for that matter.

Does that mean you don't respect him? Absolutely not. Does
that mean you don't appreciate his gifts and admire his skills?
Hardly. Respect for any God-appointed office is healthy. Without
it the church will not move forward. Respect is not only noble
and necessary, it is biblical. I think people who submit to godly
leadership and appreciate the gifts of those in ministry are mature
and discerning. You are wise to acknowledge God's hand on any
gifted minister's life, to model his example, to learn from his
instruction. All the time you learn, follow, and respect, however,
keep in mind that he is a human being like you are. Take it from
me, it is terribly uncomfortable to be treated like a king. (I should
add that it is not enjoyable to be treated like a bum, either.)

Folks in the New Testament era tried to enshrine Paul and
Barnabas. Acts 14:8–18 contains a great story. The people said,
in effect, "Zeus and Hermes have come from heaven! Look at the
miracles these men can do!" The two missionaries tore their robes
and pleaded with the people to back off. "We are men of the same
nature as you." Barnabas and Paul refused their worship. "We're
just human beings. Don't deify us! Get up off your knees!"

A few verses later, would you believe it? We read "they stoned
Paul" (14:19). Earlier they worshiped the leader, later they beat
him up and left him for dead. When I read that, I thought "good
example of the ministry." You are in the penthouse one minute
and in the outhouse the next. In the morning they are deifying
you and before dark they are stoning you. Neither extreme is
appropriate or fair.

While I am on this subject, let me give some advice to you
who are in ministry, *stay off the pedestal!* Don't get comfortable up
there. Keep crawling down. If you start liking it up there, I know
a great solution: Have a long conversation with your wife. If that
doesn't humble you, talk with your teenagers. That *never* fails to
bring the high and mighty down to earth, like fast.

Second, *remember that the flesh is weak and the adversary is strong.* Next time you doubt that, read Luke 22:31–32 where Jesus informs Peter,

> *"Simon, Simon, behold, Satan has demanded permission to sift you like wheat; but I have prayed for you, that your faith may not fail; and you, when once you have turned again, strengthen your brothers."*

Those words almost make me shudder. It is another way of saying, "The adversary is after you, Simon. You're going to fall. But when you fall, use it as an example to strengthen your brothers." Peter was the one who just said, "Though they all forsake You, I will never forsake You. Though everybody else turns away, I'll never leave you, Lord."

To every one of us in ministry, I repeat the reminder: Our flesh is weak and our adversary is real. There is not an effective, gifted minister today who is not the target of the Devil and/or his demons. Nor is there a minister strong enough in himself or herself to withstand the adversary's snare. It takes prayer. Prevailing prayer. It also takes being accountable, teachable, and open. Why? Because the enemy is so subtle. You see, no one deliberately makes *plans* to fail in the ministry. No minister ever sat on the side of his bed one morning and said, "Let's see, how can I ruin my reputation today?" But with the weakness of the flesh, mixed with the strength and reality of the adversary, failure is an ever-present possibility. Let him who thinks he stands, I repeat, take heed. . . .

Third, *release all judgment to God.* Maybe a better word is condemnation. Release all *condemnation* to God. Let Him handle all the vengeance. It is not your responsibility or mine to set every person straight. Some people have a "writing ministry of criticism." It could better be called "a ministry of vengeance." They choose various ones they want to attack, then pounce with pen in hand (and always sign it, "In Christian love"). But it is written for the purpose of cutting ministers down to size. Don't waste your time launching missiles into some brother's or sister's territory.

Leave all vengeance with God . . . He is very good at judging, you know. God is the One who started the chapter on the other person's life. He is capable of ending the chapter when He is good and ready. You are not needed to complete it. Nor am I. How easy it would be to develop a condemning and judgmental attitude in this wicked era. Let's not do it!

Finally, *refocus your attention on the ministries that are still on target.* No matter how many ministries may seem to be off the wall spiritually, very few are. Give your time, attention, and money to those God is using. Don't try to make every one just like you, by the way. This is a good time for me to say to all parishioners, let your minister be who he is . . . real. Let him be! Give him the latitude *you* want for yourself. Give him the same amount of room the grace of God affords you. Don't force him into some traditionalistic mold, requiring of him what you had in a former pastor back in 1831! Or what you read about in some great biography. Trust me, had you known that great soul better back then, you would have found something you wouldn't have liked even in him or her. Respect for those in ministry is one thing. Trying to make all ministers look alike and sound alike and please you in every way is not only unwise, it is impossible. Please . . . give us a break!

I loved Barbara Bush's comment when Barbara Walters was interviewing her on television. She said, "How do you like it when people write you and compare you to Nancy Reagan?"

The former first lady replied with unguarded candor, "I hate it."

"Why?" asked Ms. Walters.

"Because I'm Barbara Bush. I'm not Nancy. I love the Reagans, but the Reagans are no longer in the White House. I have to be who I am."

Wonderful answer!

If Mrs. Bush wants to serve wieners and sauerkraut for supper, more power to her! As the popular song goes, "I Gotta Be Me."

When it comes to ministries, look for those that square with Scripture. Look for ministers who model authenticity. Get your eyes off those who have failed and refocus your attention on those still on target . . . but (I repeat) don't try to force them into your private mold!

Be honest, okay? Have all of the ministry-related scandals caused you to turn against the Scriptures and cool off toward God? Have you begun to feel suspicious toward all churches . . . starting to look over the top of your glasses at all ministers? I've got some straight-talk advice: Don't be so critical! It is easy to get cynical in an age when nothing but bad news gets headline attention. Before long, we start judging everyone in ministry. The common reaction is, "Yep, there is another phony in the ministry." If you are fully honest, you may even have to admit, "That's why I no longer have any interest in Jesus Christ."

If that is true, I need to inform you that you are turning down the only perfect One who ever lived. Whoever you may be tempted to reject, don't reject Christ, the Lord! He is the *only* One who is absolutely perfect . . . the *only* One who can guarantee you a home in heaven. He is the *only* One who can forgive your sins. He is the *only* One who can see inside your life and separate motive from action. He is the *only* One whose death paid the debt for your sins. It is my privilege, as it has been my privilege for thirty wonderful, adventurous years to tell you that if you want to have eternal life with God, He is the *only* One who can make it happen. Give Him your life now. Hold nothing back. By faith, accept His gift today. Become one of those who stand as the Bride next to Christ. You will never regret it.

Never.

Father, thank You for the strength you have given me to write this book. It has not been easy. Convicting words have been shared. Being in the midst of an integrity crisis is a tough place to find ourselves. Authentic models of Christlikeness seem so rare. And yet, Lord, there are hundreds, even thousands, who love You and walk with You. Refocus our attention back to ministries that are getting the job done. Take away the energy-draining efforts that accompany a suspicious attitude and unforgiving spirit. Help us to live with the tension of not being able to right all the wrongs or to answer all the contradictions. Remind us of the importance of giving more attention to how we should be conducting our own lives rather than being so consumed with how others are living theirs.

Finally, dear God, wake us up! Give us courage to return to the basics rather than waste our time on low-priority nonessentials. And since our times are so wicked, so far off target, enable us to make a difference. Use us to restore respect for the ministry of the gospel. May we end this century strong.

In the matchless name of Christ I pray.

Amen.

1. If you have much contact with non-Christians (or even Christians!) on a regular basis, you will probably hear half a dozen critical, cynical remarks about the ministry within the next month or so. How will you respond? By biting your lip . . . shrugging your shoulders . . . passively nodding your head? What truths from the chapter you've just read could help you formulate a firm but non-defensive answer to unfair slurs about Christian ministry?

2. As I mentioned, I remind myself *every week of my life* that I am as capable of falling into sin and disgracing the ministry as those whose names appear in the headlines. I dare not let a week go by thinking, "It couldn't happen to me." Nor can you! What practical steps will you take to remind yourself of that fact on a weekly (or daily) basis?

3. Rather than launching a written missile at that man or woman struggling under the load of an up-front ministry, why not pen a paragraph of encouragement? (Make sure the individual doesn't have a weak heart—the shock might push 'em over the edge.) Let that slump-shouldered shepherd of yours know of your care, concern, and deep appreciation for taking the heat in a sometimes thankless but oh-so-rewarding calling.

My concern through this book has been that we not drift aim-
lessly into the twenty-first century, crossing our fingers, hoping
things work out somehow. That would be about as effective as
rearranging the deck chairs on the Titanic. There's a huge job to
be done, choice opportunities to be seized . . . and time is short.

I have not attempted to address social issues, economic
philosophies, or forms of church government within these pages.
Books abound on all of those subjects. My concern has been more
at the heart of things . . . our primary purpose as believers, our
major objectives as His church, our style of ministry, our need for
integrity. I have suggested how we might keep from losing our way
in the maze of pressure and persecution—or quenching our passion in the swamp of affluence and indifference.

This is not the only time in history when the church and its
members have forgotten that they stand beside the all-powerful
Christ as His Bride and possess all that's necessary to change the
world. The same amnesia first occurred as far back as the end of
the first century. Pen portraits of several local churches appear in
the second and third chapters of the Book of Revelation. Each
church was one a lot like yours and mine today: a lighthouse of
hope, a place where people gathered and worshiped and shared
their lives..

Although they were located on a different continent from ours
and spoke another language than we, those people were once full
of dreams, vision, and desire. Each church had its own distinc-
tives, God-given leadership, opportunities, struggles, and chal-

lenges. They knew that, as Christ's Bride, they were His representatives on the globe. And there they stood—strong citadels where truth was taught and lives were changed.

Tragically, something happened to each church that silenced its witness. Like erosion, the slippage was subtle and slow, but the same conclusion happened to all. Each finally became a shell where howling winds blew through empty sanctuaries. The strong voice of the preacher faded into silence. It was as if the Bride had walked away from the One she had stood by and was closest to. And the movement that had turned the world on its head ground to a halt.

The church at Ephesus, known for its orthodoxy, lost its warmth and ultimately its love for the Savior.

The powerful church in Pergamum began to tolerate erroneous teaching and finally became riddled with cult-like characteristics and diseased by gross immorality.

The Sardis church, so alive, active, and zealous, began to live in the past. It got to where the flock at Sardis focused only on "the way we were." Sardis became a stodgy ecclesiastical monument . . . nothing more than a morgue with a steeple.

The rich and famous Laodicean church drew great crowds, no doubt, because they never offended anybody. They had everything which led them to believe "we need nothing," yet they wound up "miserable, poor, blind, and naked." Their lukewarm style turned the Lord's stomach . . . as they too faded from the scene.

Again and again the Lord called out to His Bride. On the heels of each of the seven commentaries, the same warning appears. Seven separate times we read identical words:

> *He who has an ear, let him hear what the Spirit says to the churches!* (Revelation 2:7, 11, 17, 29; 3:6, 13, 22).

There's good reason for God to repeat Himself. He has had to call out not only to those churches but to every church, to every believer—to the Bride—in every century that has followed. He is still calling.

In the musical *Fiddler on the Roof*, Tevye, the main character, is a poor Jewish dairyman living in Russia with his wife and three daughters. Marriage is the hoped-for ideal for the three peasant girls. But because of their poverty, they can bring nothing to a match. They have no dowry. They have absolutely nothing they can offer to the one they fall in love with and want to marry.

That's the way it is with the church. We have absolutely nothing to offer Christ. Except maybe a history of bad performance reviews.

Yet this is the astounding, unbelievable, wonderful thing. Christ still wants us. And He still wants to use us.

In one of the great statements of God's purpose for Christians found anywhere in the Bible, we read "to Him be the glory in the church and in Christ Jesus to all generations forever and ever. Amen" (Ephesians 3:21). Christ and His church are to bring glory to God. It seems deliberate that the church is placed before Christ here. The meaning of the verse is that with Him beside us, Jesus believes we can do it. And not only believes we can do it, but is banking on us to do it.

And we will. Bill Hybels, founder and pastor of Willow Creek Community Church, writes:

> God can do amazing things through His people. He said He would build His church and the gates of hell would not prevail against it. Gates are defensive. We, His people, are to be on the offensive. So seek first His kingdom. Don't get entangled. Don't get choked out. Don't lose your first love of the Lord. Don't lead a lukewarm life.[44]

The central issue that will determine the church's success is not really who opposes us. It's Who's on our side. And Who we stand next to. We, the Bride, carry forth the banner of Christ. We have all the resources needed to dramatically change the world as it speeds into the twenty-first century!

Chapter 1

1. Gregory Stock, *The Book of Questions* (New York: Workman Publishing, Co., 1987), pp. 12, 15, 27, 43, 50. Reprinted by permission of Workman Publishing, Co. All rights reserved.

2. Ibid., pp. 55, 98.

3. "Westminster Shorter Catechism," *The Book of Confessions of the Presbyterian Church, USA* (New York: Office of the General Assembly, 1983), p. 7.007–.010.

4. Andrae Crouch, "My Tribute," © Lexicon Music, Inc., 1971. All rights reserved.

5. Richard H. Bube, *To Every Man An Answer: A Textbook of Christian Doctrine* (Chicago: Moody Press, 1955), p. 391.

6. From *Lee, An Abridgment* by Richard Harwell of the four-volume *R. E. Lee* by Douglas Southall Freeman. Copyright © 1961 Estate of Douglas Southall Freeman. Reprinted by permission of Charles Scribner's Sons, an imprint of Macmillan Publishing Company.

7. Anne Tyler, *Morgan's Passing* (New York: Alfred A. Knopf, 1980), quoted in *Working the Angles*, Eugene H. Peterson (Grand Rapids: Eerdmans, 1987), pp. 5–6.

Chapter 2

8. David Wiersbe and Warren W. Wiersbe, *Making Sense of the Ministry* (Grand Rapids: Baker, 1983), pp. 31–46.

9. Ibid., p. 43.

Chapter 3

10. Robert R. Shank, "Winning Over Uncertainty: Unraveling the Entanglements of Life," *Straight Talk (Living to Win Series)* (Tustin, Cal.: Priority Living, Inc., 1987).

11. Marion Jacobsen, *Saints and Snobs* (Wheaton, Ill.: Tyndale House, 1972), p. 67. Used by permission.

12. Source unknown.

Chapter 4

13. George Gallup, *Dallas Times Herald*, quoted in Fredrick Tatford, *Revelation* (Minneapolis: Klock and Klock Christian Publishing Co., 1985), p. iii–iv.

14. Walter Oetting, *The Church of the Catacombs*, rev. ed. (St. Louis, Mo.: Concordia Publishing House, 1964, 1970), p. 25.

15. Howard A. Snyder, *The Problem of Wineskins* (Downers Grove, Ill.: InterVarsity Press, 1975), pp. 75–77. Used by permission.

16. Lyle Schaller, illustrated by Edward Lee Tucker, *Looking in the Mirror* (Nashville: Abingdon, 1984), pp. 28–30.

17. John R. W. Stott, *The Preacher's Portrait* (Grand Rapids: Eerdmans, 1961), pp. 28–29.

18. Ibid., p. 30.

19. U.S. Congress. Carl Sandburg speaking before the joint session of Congress. 86th Cong., 1st sess., February 12, 1959. *Congressional Record*, vol. 105, part 2, pp. 2265–2266.

Chapter 6

20. Charles Dickens, *A Tale of Two Cities* [1859], Book I, Chapter I.

21. Denis Waitley, *Seeds of Greatness* (Old Tappan, N.J.: Revell, 1983), pp. 167–68. Used by permission.

22. Charles Wesley, "A Charge to Keep Have I," [1782].

Chapter 7

23. James Russell Lowell, "Once to Every Man and Nation," in *Familiar Quotations*, ed. John Bartlett, 15th ed. (Boston, Toronto: Little, Brown and Company Inc., 1980), p. 567.

24. John R. W. Stott, *The Message of Second Timothy* (Downers Grove, Ill.: InterVarsity Press, 1973), p. 91.

Chapter 8

25. Unpublished comment by G. Raymond Carlson during an interview with *Leadership* magazine, 20 January 1988.

26. Charles Haddon Spurgeon, quoted in Richard Ellsworth Day, *The Shadow of the Broad Brim* (Philadelphia: The Judson Press, 1934), p. 131.

27. Carl Sandburg, *Abraham Lincoln, The War Years*, vol. 4 (New York: Harcourt, Brace & Company, Inc., 1939), p. 185.

28. William Blake, "The Everlasting Gospel," *The Poetry and Prose of William Blake*, ed. David V. Erdman (Garden City, N.Y.: Doubleday & Company, Inc. Copyright by David V. Erdman and Harold Sloan, 1965), p. 512, 1.100–104.

Chapter 9

29. "An Unholy War in the TV Pulpits," *U.S. News and World Report*, 6 April 1987, p. 58.

30. *John Bartlett's Familiar Quotations*, ed. Emily Morison Beck, 15th and 125th anniversary eds., (Boston: Little Brown and Company, 1855, 1980), p. 79.

31. Ted W. Engstrom with Robert C. Larson, *Integrity* (Waco, Tex.: Word, 1987), p. 10.

32. John Gardner, *Excellence* (New York: Harper & Row, 1971), quoted in Tim Hansel, *When I Relax I Feel Guilty*, (Elgin, Ill.: David C. Cook, 1979), p. 145.

33. Martin E. Marty, "Truth: Character in Context," *Los Angeles Times*, 20 December 1987, sec. 5, p. 1, col. 1.

34. Used by permission of the author.

35. Excerpts from a letter by Charles R. Swindoll to a friend.

36. Charles Haddon Spurgeon, *Lectures to My Students* (Grand Rapids: Zondervan, 1954, 1958, 1960, 1962), pp. 13–14.

37. A. W. Tozer, *God Tells the Man Who Cares* (Harrisburg, Penn.: Christian Publications, Inc., 1970), pp. 76–79.

38. Charles R. Swindoll, *Dropping Your Guard* (Waco, Tex.: Word, 1983), pp. 168–85; *Living Above the Level of Mediocrity* (Waco, Tex.: Word, 1987), pp. 123–43.

39. Josiah Gilbert Holland, "God, Give Us Men!", quoted in *The Best Loved Poems of the American People*, selected by Hazel Felleman (Garden City, N.Y.: Garden City Books, 1936), p. 132.

Chapter 10

40. Warren W. Wiersbe, *The Integrity Crisis* (Nashville: Oliver-Nelson Books, a division of Thomas Nelson Publishers, 1988), pp. 16–17. Used by permission.

41. Chuck Colson, "Reflections on a Book Tour: It's Cold Out There," Another Point of View section, *Jubilee*, February 1988, pp. 7, 8. Used by permission of Prison Fellowship Ministries.

42. Robert Robinson, "Come, Thou Fount of Every Blessing," [1758].

43. G. Frederick Owen, *Abraham to the Middle-East Crisis*, (Grand Rapids: Eerdmans, 1939, 1957), pp. 56–57.

Conclusion

44. Bill Hybels, *Seven Wonders of the Spiritual World* (Dallas, Tex.: Word, 1988), pp. 150–51.

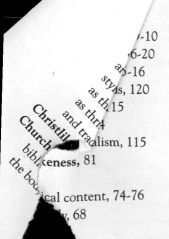

218   *SUBJECT INDEX*